P-51 Part 2
P-51D Through F-82H

P-51 Mustang

in detail & scale

Bert Kinzey

squadron/signal publications

COPYRIGHT © 1997 BY DETAIL & SCALE, INC.

All rights reserved. No part of this publication may be reproduced in any form, stored in a retrieval system, or transmitted by any means, electronic, mechanical, or otherwise, except in a review, without the written consent of the publisher.

This book is a product of Detail & Scale, Inc., which has sole responsibility for its content and layout, except that all contributors are responsible for the security clearance and copyright release of all materials submitted. Published by Squadron/Signal Publications, 1115 Crowley Drive, Carrollton, Texas 75011.

CONTRIBUTORS AND SOURCES:

Jeff Ethell	Robert Bartolacci	Jim Galloway	Frances Coutches
Lloyd Jones	Lonnie Berry	Kent Rockwell	American Aircraft Sales
Jim Roeder	Warren Munkasy	John Morgan	Rockwell Air Research
Merle Olmestead	Stan Parker	Bryce Hall	North American Aviation
David Menard	Ron Leggitt	Marilyn Hall	U. S. Air Force Museum
Bill Slatton	Josh Hairston	John MacGuire	War Eagles Museum, Santa Teresa, New Mexico
Walt Fink	Helge Lind	Betty MacGuire	Yanks Air Museum, Chino, California
Al Lloyd	Goran Ahlatrom	Mike Coutches	Planes of Fame Museum, Chino, California

Many photographs in this publication are credited to their contributors. Photographs with no credit indicated were taken by the author.

Detail & Scale, Inc., and the author express a special word of thanks to Jim Roeder who spent a lot of time taking photographs, building and reviewing model kits, and providing valuable information for this publication.

Sincere appreciation is also extended to John and Betty MacGuire of the War Eagles Museum at Santa Teresa, New Mexico. The museum's beautifully restored Mustangs were made available to Detail & Scale, Inc., for detailed photography during the research and preparation of this book. Their help and cooperation significantly enhanced the detailed coverage provided in this publication. Detail & Scale, Inc., and the author encourage all aviation enthusiasts to visit and support this outstanding museum.

Front cover photo: "BUTCH BABY" was Jullian H. Bertram's Mustang, and it was assigned to the 357th Fighter Group. P-51Ds were delivered in a natural metal and silver dope finish, but the 357th FG painted many of its P-51Ds in the field. At times regulation USAAF Olive Drab and Neutral Gray were used, but British greens and grays were often used as well. "BUTCH BABY" was painted with British Dark Green over U. S. Neutral Gray. The small orange object with the silver surround on the side of the fuselage is a formation light. A second light was located near the center of the national insignia. This aircraft also appears in the background of the top photograph on page 33, and the light within the national insignia can be seen in that photo. Formation lights were also on the opposite side of the fuselage, but they were installed on relatively few Mustangs. Note also that this aircraft is fitted with the AN/APS-13 tail warning radar antenna which remains natural metal.
(Sloan via Kuhnert and Ethell)

Rear cover, top photo: The instrument panel in the P-51D differed little from previous Mustang variants.

Rear cover, bottom photo: Colors and details of the Merlin engine in a P-51D are illustrated in this vintage World War II color photo. *(Ethell collection)*

INTRODUCTION

The large three-blade propeller on this Mustang confirms that this is one of three XP-51Fs which were evaluated during 1944. (USAFM)

This volume in the Detail & Scale Series completes our two-part coverage of the P-51 Mustang and P/F-82 Twin Mustang. Volume 50, entitled The P-51 Mustang in Detail & Scale, Part 1, covered all Mustang variants up through the P-51C. This title includes the remaining P-51 versions and all variants of the P/F-82 Twin Mustang.

In order to illustrate the physical details of these aircraft in more detail than ever previously provided in any aviation publication, several trips were made by three different photographers to take scores of photographs specifically for this publication. Each of these photographers is also a modeler, and each took photographs that best illustrate the features a modeler would want to see. All three also built and reviewed kits for the Modelers Section at the end of this book.

A beautiful P-51D at the War Eagles Museum in Santa Teresa, New Mexico, has been restored to factory standards, and this was photographed by the author and Bill Slatton. Bill also photographed that museum's TP-51D. The author traveled to Chino, California, Dayton, Ohio, Washington, D. C., and Warner Robins, Georgia, to photograph other vintage aircraft that have been restored or preserved. An effort has been made to include photographs which accurately illustrate the details as they appeared when the aircraft were operational.

Jim Roeder made two trips to photograph one of the two P-51Hs that remain in flyable condition. Included in this volume are many of his photos which illustrate the unique features of this Mustang variant in greater detail than ever published before. The P-82B at the Air Force Museum was also photographed in detail by the author, and five pages of detailed photos of that aircraft are also included. An additional color page illustrates the cockpits in this famous aircraft. Overall, there is a total of twenty-eight pages of detailed photographs, most of which were taken specifically for this publication.

Well known aviation researcher, author, and artist, Lloyd Jones, created original line drawings in 1/72nd scale specifically for this Detail & Scale book. Multiple views are included for the P-51D/K, P-51H, and the P/F-82 Twin Mustang. These were based on official drawings and plating diagrams from North American Aviation. As far as we know, the drawings of the Twin Mustang are the first ever made available to the general public that show the correct location of the trailing edge on the center wing section. Lloyd has provided a total of eight and one-half pages of 1/72nd scale drawings which clearly illustrate the design and features of each variant. The major differences between the versions are also indicated on the drawings.

Our Modelers Section provides comprehensive reviews of the kits available to the scale modeler for these Mustang variants. All standard scales ranging from 1/144th to 1/24th are included.

This two-volume detailed look at all Mustang and Twin Mustang variants was made possible through the efforts of many people who contributed their time, knowledge, photographs, and efforts. Their names appear on page 2 of this book and Volume 50. Detail & Scale, Inc., and the author express a sincere word of thanks to each of them.

DEVELOPMENTAL HISTORY

The two round mirrors above the canopy of this P-51D appear to be the eyes of an insect, but they were important in helping the pilot check his six-o'clock position. "Tar Heel" was flown by Kirke Everson who was credited with only 1.5 aerial victories. However, Everson destroyed thirteen German aircraft on the ground to lead the 504th Fighter Squadron in this category. The 504th FS was one of the squadrons of the 339th Fighter Group, and it used 6N fuselage codes. The checks on the nose are red and white. *(USAFM)*

By mid-1944, P-51 Mustangs were fast replacing other types of fighters in the USAAF. The early variants with Allison powerplants were combat veterans and had proven to be superior in performance over any other allied fighter below 15,000 feet. The Merlin-powered P-51B and P-51C possessed outstanding high altitude performance that made them formidable adversaries to any enemy aircraft above 12,000 feet. Additionally, all Mustang variants had great range capabilities which exceeded most other fighter aircraft of World War II.

But as good as the Mustang was, there were several problems with the design, and complaints about two shortcomings in particular resulted in the development of the P-51D and subsequent versions. First, the visibility from the original standard canopy was very restricted. In combat, the pilot who saw his adversary first had a decided advantage, and more often than not, the first indication a fighter pilot had that he was under attack was the impact of bullets on his aircraft. Although the British Malcolm canopy had been fitted to many early Mustangs, it was an interim solution which was not available in sufficient quantities for all aircraft.

The second complaint about the Mustang that required correcting was that the four .50-caliber machine guns were not sufficient for the average pilot. Further, they were subject to jamming, and this was due in part because they were mounted at an angle.

To correct the visibility problem, two P-51Bs were modified with a cut down, aft fuselage section and a full bubble canopy. This provided excellent visibility all around and above the aircraft. Beginning with the P-51D and the nearly identical P-51K, all future Mustang variants were designed and fitted with full bubble canopies.

For more firepower, the number of machine guns was

Because of complaints about the limited visibility of the standard framed canopy used on early Mustang variants, P-51B, 43-12102, was modified with a cut down aft fuselage and a full bubble canopy. It was used as a test aircraft for what became the P-51D and P-51K. *(NAA via Jones)*

Lt. William "Hank" Gruber leads P-51Ds from the 357th Fighter Group in "Cooter." The name was painted on both sides of the aircraft in red letters which had a yellow outline. This particular aircraft was painted British Dark Green over U. S. Neutral Gray.
(USAFM)

increased from four to six. This was a rather simple matter, because the gun bays in previous Mustangs had always been large enough for an extra gun in each wing. To reduce chances of jamming, the guns were mounted upright instead of at a slant. Additionally, they were installed along the dihedral of the wing rather than being parallel to the ground line as they were in earlier variants. The P-51D and all subsequent production versions had six internal machine guns. Ammunition capacities for the guns were also increased, and a K-14B gyro-computing gunsight replaced the reflector sights during the P-51D production run.

During the second half of 1944, P-51Ds and P-51Ks were arriving in both the European and Pacific Theaters in considerable numbers. Although they served in combat during World War II for less than a year, their numbers exceeded all previous versions combined. They scored impressively against all types of enemy aircraft, although admittedly, the German and Japanese air forces were significantly reduced in both quality and quantity during the last twelve months of combat.

Even the early versions of the Mustangs were considered to have substantial eye appeal with their sleek aerodynamic lines, due in part to the streamlined nose which housed the inline, liquid-cooled, engine. But with the introduction of the bubble canopy on the P-51D and P-51K, there were few who would argue that these Mustangs were not among the most handsome fighter designs ever produced. This undoubtedly lead to the Mustang's overall popularity among pilots and aviation enthusiasts alike.

In the air, the Mustang could hold its own against any other propeller-driven aircraft of World War II. But in the closing months of the war, particularly in Europe, there were decreasing opportunities for aerial combat with enemy fighters. Instead, allied fighters were used more and more for strafing missions against the German army on the ground, airfields, rail yards, and other ground targets. These were usually well defended by a considerable number of anti-aircraft weapons ranging from machine guns to the famous German 88-mm gun. A single hit to the liquid cooling system would bring a Mustang down, and because the critical components of this cooling system were in the forward and lower sections of the fuselage, the Mustang proved more vulnerable to ground fire than it was to enemy aircraft. As a result, the ratio of losses to missions flown was higher on these ground attack missions for the P-51 than they were for the P-47 Thunderbolt with its air-cooled engine. The vulnerability of the liquid-cooled engine to ground fire would surface again as a problem for the F-51D in Korea where losses were very high.

In addition to the United States, at least twenty-two foreign nations also operated Mustangs at some point in time. While some of these flew P-51s in combat during World War II, others used them in smaller air forces as late as the 1970s. Australia built eighty P-51Ds which were designated CA-17s and called Mustang Mk XX. An additional batch of 106 aircraft built in Australia were designated CA-18s. They were called Mustang Mk XXI, XXII, and XXIII depending on the engine used and the equipment fitted. A Mustang Mk XXII is shown here.
(USAFM)

The P-51H also served after the war with the USAF and the Air National Guard. These P-51Hs are assigned to the 64th Fighter Squadron of the 57th Fighter Group.
(USAFM)

Produced too late for service in World War II, the P-82/F-82 Twin Mustang served post-war as both a long range fighter and a radar-equipped, all-weather interceptor/night fighter.
(NAA via Jones)

The P-51D and the very similar P-51K became operational in considerable numbers during the final year of World War II, and they were the final Mustang variants to fly combat missions in that war. Although the production lines had already begun deliveries of the P-51H prior to the end of hostilities, none reached operational units in time to participate in combat. Because it was considerably lighter, the P-51H offered a significant increase in performance over the P-51D and P-51K, and the center of balance problem was finally corrected. In the early post-war years, the P-51H became the Mustang of choice for the USAAF and then the USAF, while the P-51Ds were the first to be turned over to the Air National Guard. But as the new jets replaced more and more propeller-driven fighters, even the P-51Hs were sent to Guard units.

During World War II, the Pacific theater posed a far different set of problems than those in Europe. The vast expanses of the Pacific Ocean were fine for carrier-based aircraft, but it was a foregone conclusion that it was going to be difficult to provide land-based fighter escort for USAAF bombers during missions over the Japanese homeland. Studies to increase the range of existing fighters and to develop new long-range fighters were conducted to address this problem. One result was the P-47N version of the Thunderbolt which had a maximum range of 2,200 miles. This put it in the same range category as the P-51D. But these missions to Japan and back were of such long duration, pilot fatigue was also a critical problem.

North American Aviation addressed this problem with the development of the P-82. Although this Twin Mustang offered a range increase of only 300 miles over the P-51D, this could be critical on these escort missions. But even more important was the fact that the P-82 had two pilots who could relieve each other on these extended missions.

The capture of Iwo Jima proved to be the real solution for providing fighter escort to the B-29s over Japan. Not only could fighters be based on Iwo Jima, but it could serve as an emergency base for crippled bombers returning from Japan as well. P-51Ds were quite capable of providing escort from this important airstrip, while P-47Ns flew from Ie Shima.

By the time the war ended, only twenty P-82Bs had been delivered, and none ever flew a combat mission during that war. Production was severely cut back, and 100 P-82Es became the first Twin Mustang variant to reach operational service in any strength. They did serve as the Strategic Air Command's first escort fighter, and they could be used as heavily armed ground attack aircraft as well. But it was in the all-weather or night fighting role where the P-82 was used in the greatest numbers. With the designation change from P-82 to F-82 in 1948, F-82F, G, and H versions entered service as all-weather interceptors/night fighters with the air defense forces of the United States Air Force. They saw limited operational use in Korea where one scored the first USAF aerial victory of

When the USAAF became the United States Air Force in 1948, Mustangs were redesignated F-51s. Here F-51s are shown in U. S. Air Force markings during the Korean War period. (Ethell)

F-51Ds saw combat again in the skies over Korea. At left, a quad-.50 machine gun mount provides anti-aircraft protection for Mustangs on an airfield in South Korea. In the photograph at right, "OL' N₈DS₀B" looks more like a seaplane as it sloshes through the huge mud puddles at Chinhae, Korea, in 1951. This F-51D was assigned to the 67th Fighter-Bomber Squadron and was flown By Robert "Pancho" Pasqualicchio. Pasqualicchio had previously flown Thunderbolts and was one of many pilots who would have preferred P-47s for ground support in Korea. Mustangs used in this role had a very high loss rate, and during World War II, Thunderbolts had proved more survivable in the face of the intense ground fire often experienced on these missions. (Left Jones, right USAFM)

the war.

But it was the P-51D variant that again saw considerable combat during the Korean War. Having been redesignated the F-51D in 1948, they attacked targets on the ground with rockets, bombs, and machine guns, often with more success than the early jet fighters then in use. But the Mustang, with its liquid cooled engine, again proved very vulnerable to ground fire, and as a result, loss rates for these missions were very high. Former Thunderbolt pilots longed to have their big air-cooled, radial-engined fighters for this dangerous low level work.

The use of the F-51D in Korea was a result of Air Force philosophy which favored three types of fighters. These included the basic air superiority fighter like the F-86, the all-weather fighter-interceptor like the F-94, and the fighter-bomber like the F-84. Each of these types took part in the air war over Korea. But nowhere in Air Force thinking was the attack aircraft considered. This contrasted with the Navy's approach which provided A1D Skyraiders for this specific purpose. Radial-engined F4U Corsairs also proved far more survivable than Mustangs in the ground attack role, and they could carry a heavier load. Simply stated, the F-51D was the only propeller-driven fighter-bomber available to the Air Force in quantity. Unfortunately, the Air Force failed to learn from this lesson in Korea. It was later forced to obtain Navy Skyraiders for use in Vietnam as well as buy its own version of the Navy-designed A-7 Corsair II for use in that war. Only then did the Air Force develop its first dedicated attack aircraft, the A-10 Thunderbolt.

This is not to say that the Mustang did not make a worthy contribution to the war in Korea. F-51Ds, and the pilots that flew them, performed their jobs well. But unfortunately, they did so in the face of very high losses.

Over the years since the retirement of the last Mustang from Air National Guard service, several attempts have been made to return Mustangs to service. Certainly, the most significant of these were made by the Cavalier Aircraft Corporation which developed both piston and turbo-prop versions as counter-insurgency aircraft. Two modified F-51Ds returned briefly to the Army's inventory when they were used in the Cheyenne helicopter tests.

Without question, the P-51 Mustang was one of the great aircraft designs of all times. It will forever be considered a classic among all aircraft ever built. But a disservice has been paid to it by those who would make unrealistic claims about its performance and contributions to the victory in World War II. Often, the word "best" has

The 10,000th Mustang built was autographed by North American employees and is shown at left. At right, Gwen Knox Hurst adds her name to the left side of the fuselage of the final P-51D which was also autographed by those who helped build it. (Hurst via USAFM)

The Air National Guard also operated Mustangs in considerable numbers. These F-51Ds are assigned to the Kentucky Air National Guard. (USAFM)

been attributed to the Mustang. But "best" must be qualified to the point that it becomes practically meaningless. When applied to a fighter aircraft, "best" is usually related to performance figures. Certainly, the Me-262 jet fighter was superior in many ways to the Mustang, so it is often written that the Mustang was the best propeller-driven fighter ever built. But the Germans had several types of propeller-driven fighters under development that were clearly superior, and the U. S. Navy's F8F Bearcat proved to be a much better fighter in almost every respect except range. So the claim is made that it was the best propeller-driven fighter that served in World War II, or sometimes this is even further qualified to state that it was the best propeller-driven allied fighter of the war. Very justifiable arguments can be made that the P-47 Thunderbolt or the F4U Corsair were better in some respects or even overall, but it is really not possible to objectively call any one fighter the best of World War II.

Likewise, it has been written that the P-51 was the fighter that "won the war." This is also a ludicrous contention. Everyone from generals to the man on the street have claimed that one weapon or another won the war. Eisenhower said that the artillery won the war. Many have said that the atomic bomb won the war, or the aircraft carrier did, or the heavy bomber did. No weapon won the war. The war was won by people. This included the soldier with a rifle, the driver of a tank, the sailor on a ship, and the pilot and crewmen in an aircraft. It included the people that built the machines and weapons of war and those who delivered this equipment to the ones who used them. It included the people who made the decisions and dictated the tactics, and it included the ones that carried them out.

Of the machines and weapons of war, some played a more important part than others, and indeed, a few played a very critical part. But it was a combination of all of them that resulted in victory. No single weapon system decided the outcome of the entire war. Many credit the Mustang with winning the war in Europe, because it had the range to escort the bombers all the way to their targets in the heartland of Germany. But this capability was always there, even before the P-51 became available. The fact that long range fighters were not used earlier was a tactical decision rather than because such fighters did not exist. This is discussed in greater detail in The P-51 Mustang in Detail & Scale, Part 1.

Was the Mustang's contribution more important than that of the Spitfires and Hurricanes that defended England in 1940 and preserved that country as a base from which to fight the German war machine? Other similar examples could also be cited, but the point is that it is a disservice to both the Mustang and to the other weapon systems that contributed so much to the war, to claim that any one of them "won the war."

Just as the Mustang is and always will be one of the best fighter designs ever developed and a classic in aviation history, its contribution to the war effort was indeed significant. But the highest praise that can be bestowed upon this aircraft and all of the designers, pilots, and ground crew associated with it, is to tell the honest and accurate story of its performance and its contributions throughout its operational service. When this is done, the Mustang will stand tall on its own true merits. These are significant and remarkable enough that they don't need any further embellishment from claims and statements that cannot be substantiated in reality.

The last Mustang in U. S. service was this F-51D. It is shown here as it was delivered to the USAF Museum by Major James Miller of the West Virginia Air National Guard. This aircraft remains on display in the museum today. (USAFM)

MUSTANG VARIANTS
P-51D & P-51K (MUSTANG IV)

*"Double Trouble" was a P-51D assigned to the 352nd Fighter Squadron of the 353rd Fighter Group. Fuselage codes were SX*B, and the checks were yellow and black. Four kill markings are painted below the canopy rail. (USAFM)*

A total of 6,502 P-51Ds were built at North American's plant in California, while an additional 1,600 were produced in Dallas, Texas. These Dallas-built aircraft were originally to be called P-51Es, but the designation was changed to P-51D before production began. This was because the USAAF opted simply to rely on North American's NA suffix for the aircraft produced in California and NT for identical examples built in Texas. This change eliminated the use of different model letters for the same variant just because some were from one production line and others were produced elsewhere. This had previously been the case for the identical P-51B and P-51C.

The combined total of 8,102 P-51Ds exceeded by a wide margin the production numbers for any other Mustang variant. Of the 1,600 P-51Ds built in Texas, 136 were fitted with cameras and redesignated as F-6D photo reconnaissance versions. Initially ten P-51D-25-NTs were built as two-seat trainers, but fifteen more were modified in 1951. P-51D-25-NT, 44-84900, was converted for carrier trials and redesignated ETF-51D-25-NT.

The P-51K, which was nearly identical to the P-51D, was also built in Dallas, and production for this version totaled 1,500. Of all P-51Ds and P-51Ks built in the United States, 280 P-51Ds and 594 P-51Ks went to the Royal Air Force where they were both called Mustang IV. Of the remaining 906 P-51Ks, 163 were completed as reconnaissance aircraft, and they received the F-6K designation.

Two hundred P-51Ds were built under license in Australia and were designated C17s and C18s. They were called Mustang Mk 20, 21, 22, and 23 depending on the engine and equipment installed. Although these entered service too late for action in World War II, they did see combat during the Korean War.

The main difference between the P-51D and P-51K was the propeller used. Initially, the P-51D used the Hamilton Standard cuffed propeller that was 11'2" in diameter. The P-51K was fitted with an Aeroproducts uncuffed propeller of 11'0" in diameter. This hollow-blade prop was to prove troublesome, and up to one in five were rejected due to vibration problems. Later in their service life, P-51Ds were fitted with an uncuffed Hamilton Standard propeller with blunt tips.

There were two types of canopies used on the P-51D and P-51K. One, with a continuous smooth curve, is usually associated with the P-51D, while the other, with a higher profile and a noticeable increase in curvature near the aft end, is normally connected with the P-51K. While initial production may have often divided the two canopies in this manner, the fact is that both types fitted both versions of the Mustang, and each was commonly seen on both variants. Canopies of both types were regularly used as replacements on both the P-51D and P-51K in the field.

The two major improvements that the P-51D and P-51K offered over all previous Mustangs were the improved visibility due to the bubble canopy and the greater firepower of six .50-caliber machine guns. Only four guns had been installed in the P-51A, P-51B, and P-51C.

P-51Ds and P-51Ks which were fitted with cameras were redesignated F-6Ds and F-6Ks respectively. This designation was subsequently changed to FP-51D at the same time the P-51D designation was changed to F-51 in 1948. At left is an in-flight view of an F-6D named "Gonzales." The close-up at right shows the camera installation. There were two cameras mounted horizontally in the aft fuselage, and one vertical camera. The lens port for the vertical camera is just forward of the tail wheel. *(Both USAFM)*

Other less noticeable changes included a redesigned wing with a large fillet at the leading edge root. The navigation lights on the wings were changed to a single light on each wing tip. Earlier versions had a light on the top and the bottom of each wing near the tip. The landing/taxi lights, which had always been mounted in the leading edge of the wing on previous variants, were now located inside the wheel wells. They hung down from the back of the wells when the gear was down, and were pushed up inside the wells when the gear retracted.

The design of the main gear wells and inner doors changed slightly from the earlier Mustangs, and there were other minor modifications as well. But otherwise the basic and proven design of the fighter remained the same as it had been on the P-51B and P-51C.

Another change to the P-51D and P-51K came about after these two variants had entered service. Problems with directional stability were compounded by the cut down, aft fuselage area. To reduce this problem, a fillet was added between the leading edge of the vertical tail and the spine of the aircraft. Not only was this fillet added on the production lines, many Mustangs in the field had it retrofitted to include a few P-51Bs and P-51Cs.

The P-51D and P-51K, as well as their camera-laden counterparts, began to reach operational service during the second half of 1944. Their numbers increased rapidly over the last year of the war, and by war's end, Mustangs had become the most numerous of all fighter types in service with the USAAF. Total Mustang production was second only to the P-47 Thunderbolt among all U. S. fighters produced during World War II.

Although the subsequent P-51H offered increased performance, it was the P-51D that became the best known and most popular of all Mustang variants. It was exported to almost two dozen foreign nations, and of all versions that had served in World War II, it was the F-51D that saw combat again in Korea. An F-51D also became the last propeller-driven fighter to see service with the Air National Guard. The very last F-51D in U. S. service was retired by the West Virginia Air National Guard to permanent display at the U. S. Air Force Museum in Dayton, Ohio, where it remains today.

Beginning on the next page are four pages of drawings and fifteen pages of detailed photographs that illustrate the features of the P-51D and P-51K. Most were taken specifically for this publication. In the color gallery are detailed photographs of the engine, cockpit, and gun bays.

Mechanics in the Republic of Korea Air Force perform maintenance on an F-51D. *(USAFM)*

Many F-51Ds served with the Air National Guard. This aircraft flew with the Tennessee Guard. *(USAFM)*

P-51D & P-51K DIMENSIONS

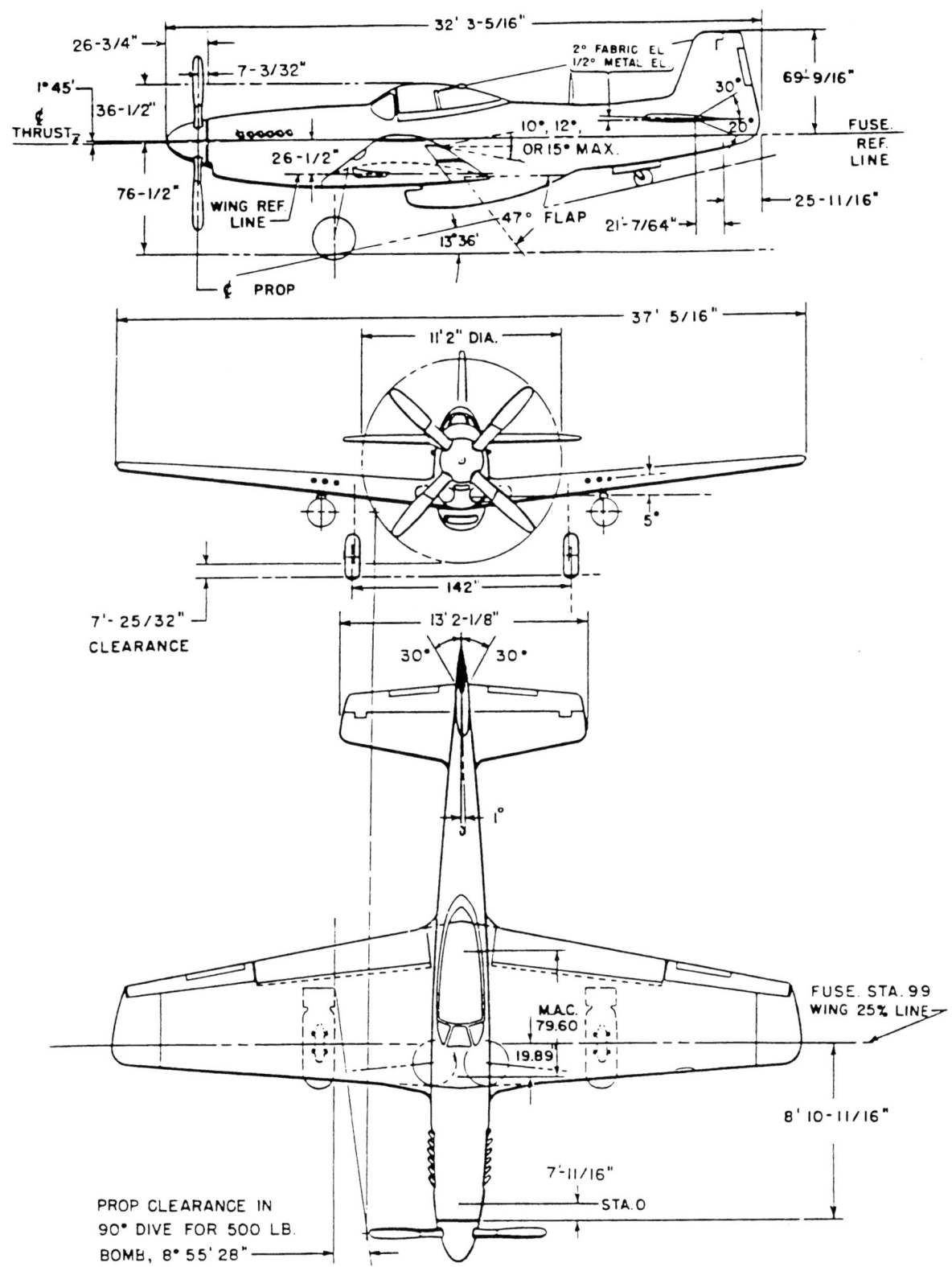

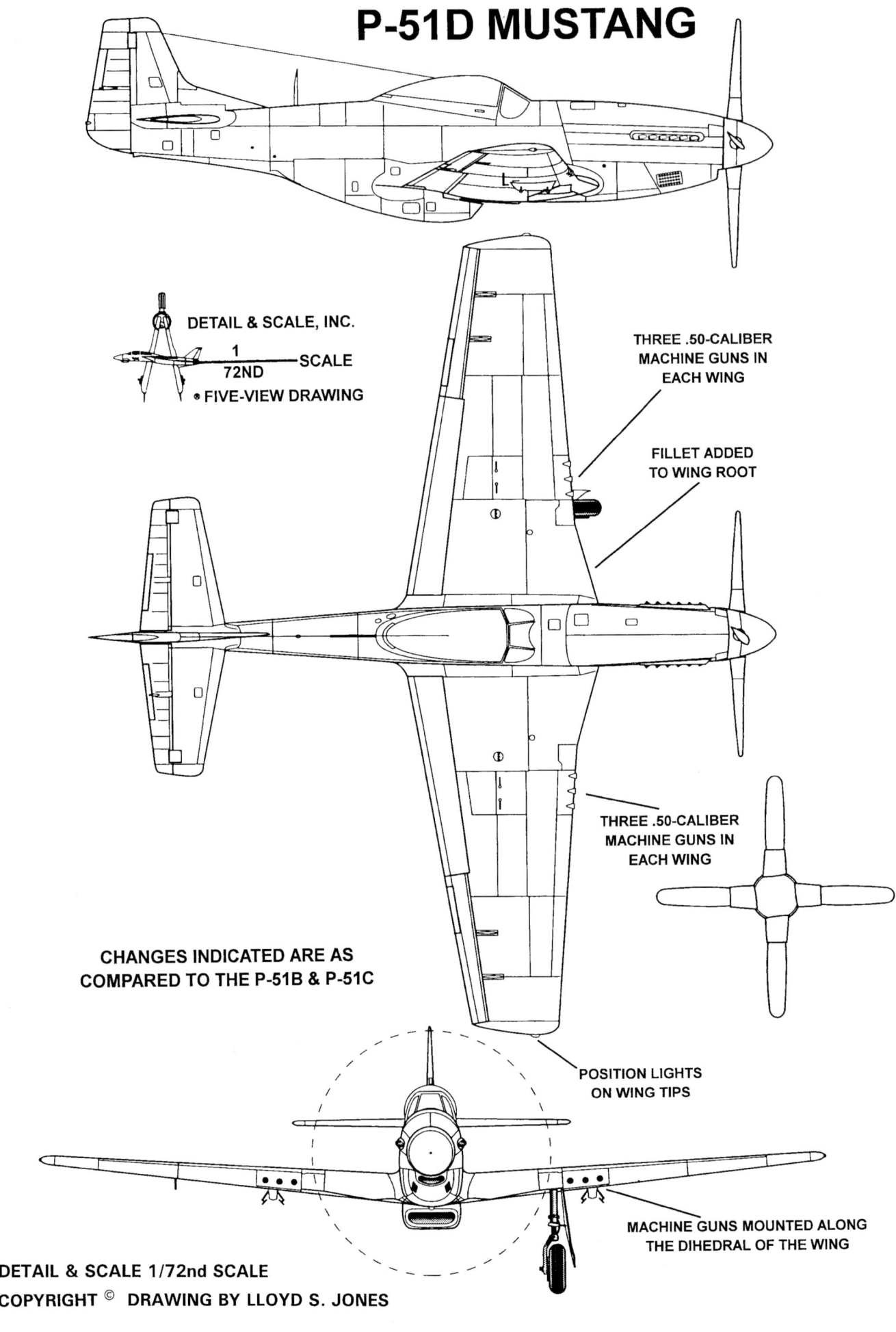

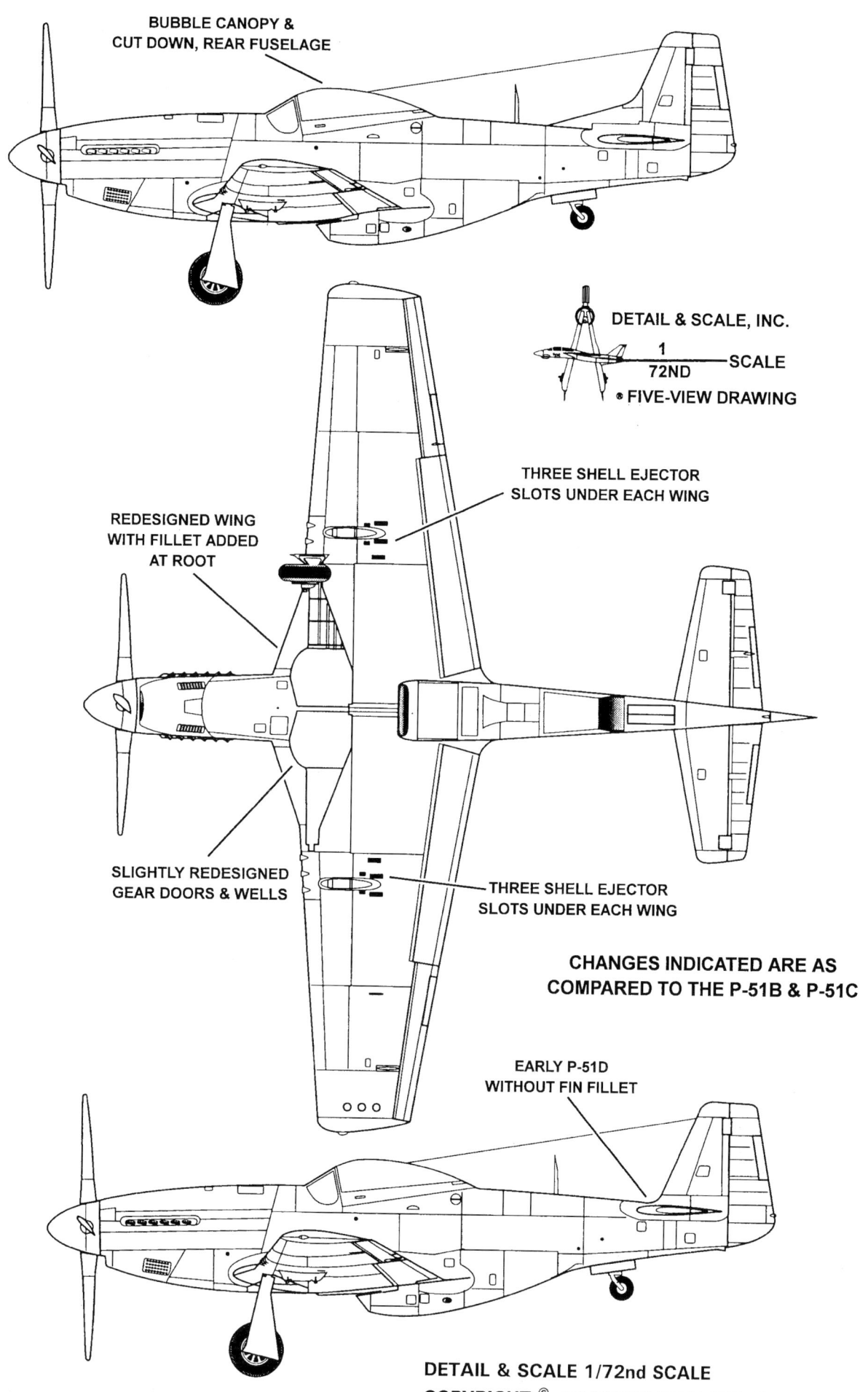

13

F-6D PHOTO-RECONNAISSANCE VARIANT

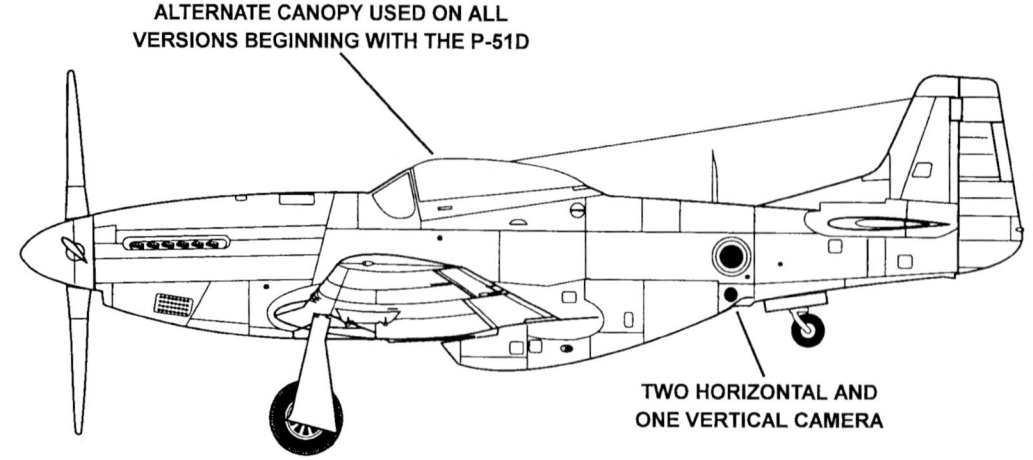

ALTERNATE CANOPY USED ON ALL VERSIONS BEGINNING WITH THE P-51D

TWO HORIZONTAL AND ONE VERTICAL CAMERA

TP-51D TWO-SEAT TRAINER

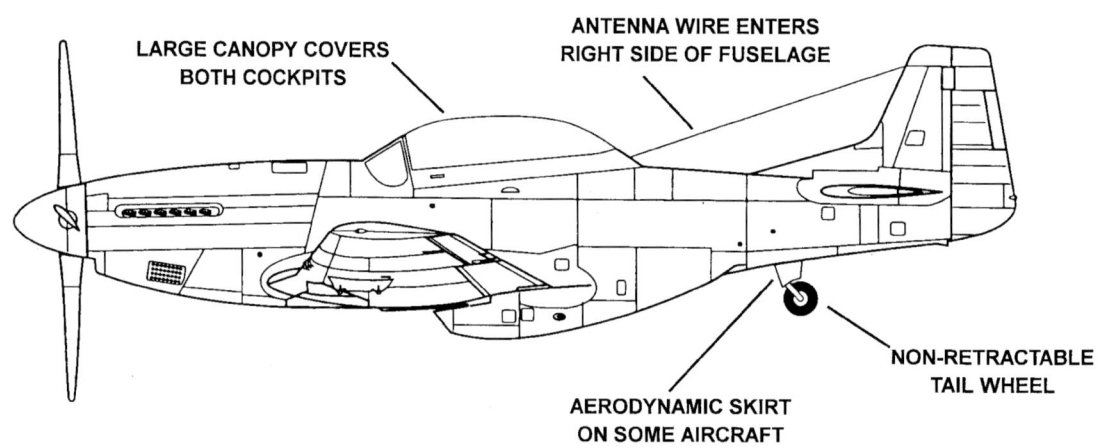

LARGE CANOPY COVERS BOTH COCKPITS

ANTENNA WIRE ENTERS RIGHT SIDE OF FUSELAGE

AERODYNAMIC SKIRT ON SOME AIRCRAFT

NON-RETRACTABLE TAIL WHEEL

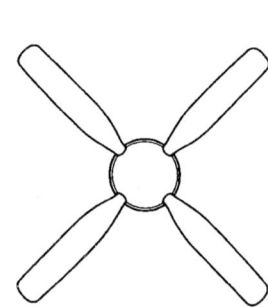

HAMILTON STANDARD CUFFLESS PROPELLER USED ON P/F-51Ds LATE IN THEIR OPERATIONAL SERVICE

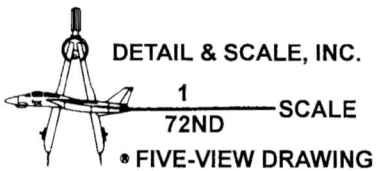

DETAIL & SCALE, INC.
1/72ND SCALE
FIVE-VIEW DRAWING

110-GALLON EXTERNAL TANK

DETAIL & SCALE 1/72nd SCALE COPYRIGHT © DRAWING BY LLOYD S. JONES

PROPELLERS

Above: P-51Ds were originally fitted with a cuffed Hamilton Standard hydromatic propeller with rounded tips as shown on "Is This Trip Necessary?." This P-51D was assigned to the 506th Fighter Group, and it was photographed after a mission over Tokyo on 28 May, 1945. The left landing gear partially collapsed when the aircraft made a hard landing on Bonin Island.   (USAFM)

Right: This close-up shows the details and shape of one of the propeller blades of the cuffed Hamilton Standard propeller. The propeller was 11'2" in diameter.

Above: P-51Ks were fitted with an Aeroproducts A-542-A unimatic propeller that did not have cuffs. It was eleven feet in diameter, thus being two inches less than the Hamilton Standard cuffed propeller. This particular P-51K has been fitted with cameras for the tactical reconnaissance role. Reconnaissance P-51Ks were designated F-6K-NT.   (USAFM)

Left: The design of the Aeroproducts propeller can be seen here.

Later, many P-51Ds were fitted with a non-cuffed Hamilton Standard propeller with blunt tips. Some of these had deicing provisions, while others did not. This style of propeller was often seen on post-war P-51Ds, and they were used extensively during the Korean war.

PYLONS & EXTERNAL STORES

 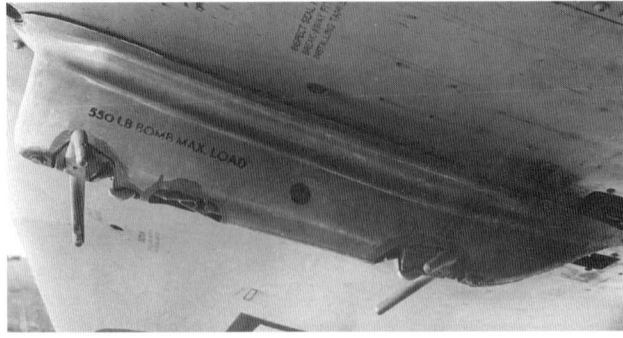

There was a single pylon under each wing of all single-engine Mustangs beginning with the P-51A and A-36. At left is an outboard view of the pylon under the left wing, and at right is an inboard view of the pylon under the right wing. (Left author, right USAFM)

Metal, 75-gallon tanks had a teardrop shape. At left is a look at two tanks ready to be attached to the pylon. At right is a tank mounted on the right pylon. Note the plumbing running between the tank and the aircraft. (USAFM)

The other tank commonly seen on Mustangs during World War II had a capacity of 110 gallons. It was made partially of compressed paper, and was often referred to as the paper tank.

In the post-war era, other tanks were sometimes carried on Mustangs, particularly on ferry missions. At left is one style of these tanks on a Minnesota ANG P-51D, while at right is a tank very similar to the one used on the wing tips of the F-80 Shooting Star. (USAFM)

Both bombs and rockets could be delivered from underwing stations. This photograph shows a P-51D fitted with both types of weapons during armament tests in November 1944.
(USAFM)

Beginning in December 1944 on the Texas production lines, and in January 1945 at California, zero-length rocket stubs were added under the wings of P-51s. Provisions to carry three five-inch rockets under each wing was standard.

This test aircraft is shown with five rockets under each wing. The inboard two rockets in each case are attached to launchers on the standard pylon.
(USAFM)

Triple-tube launchers for 4.5-inch rockets were also evaluated for use on the Mustang, but were more commonly seen on P-47 Thunderbolts.
(USAFM)

This P-51D is equipped with practice bomb dispensers on its pylons.
(USAFM)

LANDING GEAR DETAILS

Details of the right main landing gear are visible here. The landing gear on the P-51D and P-51K was identical, but it had detail differences when compared to all earlier versions. It was also considerably different from the P-51H which followed. (See page 46.) Particularly note the shape of the outer gear door and the details of the outer wheel hub in this photograph.

Details of the inner wheel hub are revealed in this close-up. There is a tow ring at the end of the strut.

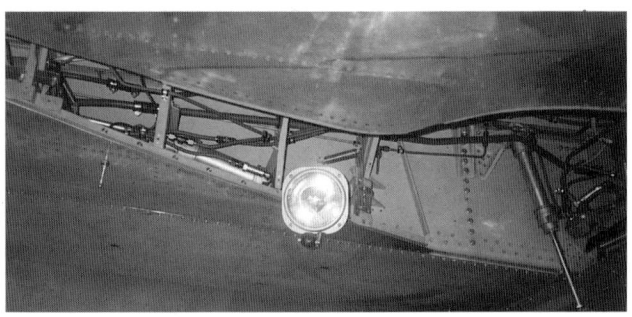

While earlier P-51s variants had landing/taxi lights mounted in the leading edges of their wings, the lights on the P-51D and -K were mounted in the wheel wells. They had a wooden roller at the bottom, and the outer gear door pushed against this roller thus folding the light up into the well when the gear retracted. These lights were only in the left wheel well on some aircraft, and in both wells on others. This one is mounted in the right well of a late production P-51D.

This view from the front shows the correct alignment of the strut and the outer door. (Slatton)

This view looks up and toward the aircraft's centerline inside the right wheel well. Official USAAF specifications called for the interior of the well to be painted Chromate Yellow primer.

The right main gear is shown here. The strut was usually painted a flat silver or steel color. The interior of the outer door was usually not painted with a primer.

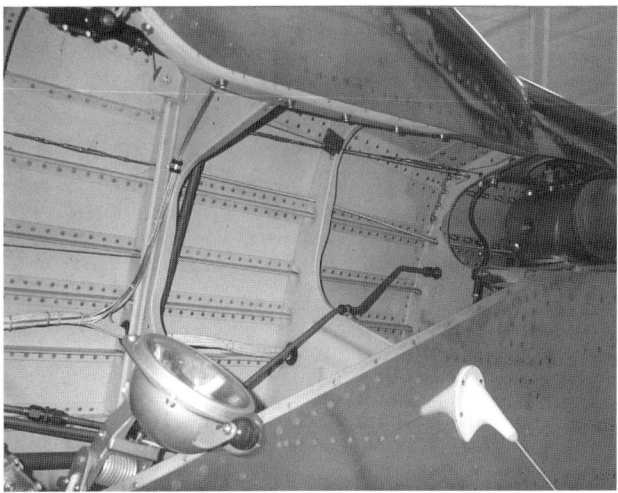

The interior of the left main gear well is shown in this view that looks almost straight up into the well.

This is the forward part of the left main gear well. Note the two lightening holes in the forward wall. The black box inside the hole to the right is the gun camera.

The actuator for the inner main gear door can be seen here. Note that it is at the aft end of the well and door. It was at the forward end of the well and door on the earlier versions and on the subsequent P-51H.

This view also was taken inside the left main landing gear well, and it looks up and in toward the center of the aircraft.

Details of the inner main gear doors are shown here. When the engine was shut down, the hydraulic pressure would hold these doors in the up position. But as the pressure gradually bled off, the doors would drop to this lowered position.

Above and below: The tail wheel was retractable and was supported by a strut on only one side of the wheel.

The rectangular tail wheel doors were actuated by rods at the aft end. The interior of the tail wheel well was painted Chromate Yellow primer, but the insides of the doors were usually left unpainted.

WING DETAILS

Internal armament consisted of three .50-caliber machine guns in each wing. They were mounted in a slightly staggered arrangement, and spent shells were ejected through slots under the wing. The three slots under the right wing can be seen in the background aft of the pylon.

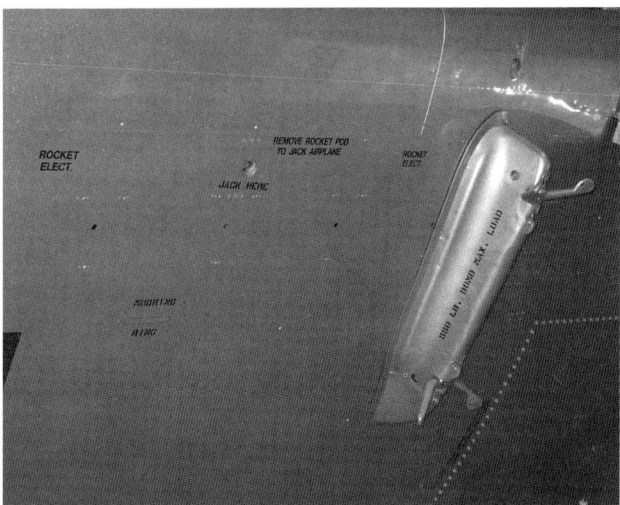

Details just outboard of the pylon are illustrated here. There is a jack point as indicated by the stenciling, and a retractable mooring ring is located further aft. By pushing on one end of the ring, the other end moved downward and exposed the circular ring area where a rope or chain could be attached. (Slatton)

At left is a top view of the gun muzzles in the left wing. The slightly staggered arrangement is visible, with the outboard gun being the furthest forward. At right are the same guns shown from the front. Unlike the earlier Mustang variants, these guns were mounted in line with the dihedral of the wing rather than being parallel to the ground line. Note how the inboard gun is recessed into the wing. A blast tube extends from the muzzle to a point just forward of the leading edge of the wing.

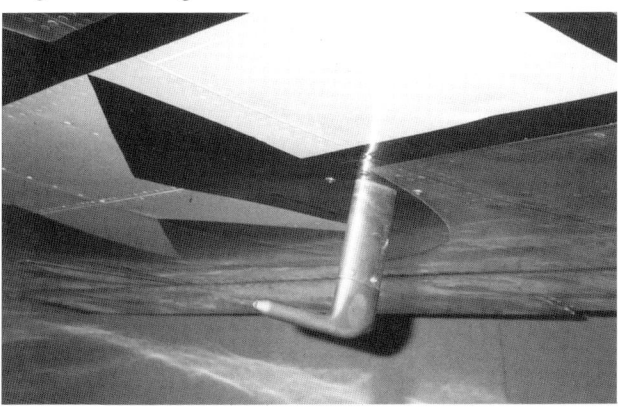

Like all other Mustang variants except the A-36, the P-51D and -K had an L-shaped pitot probe under the right wing. It is shown here from the inside looking outward.

The gun camera opening was located in the leading edge of the left wing near the root.

The latches on the forward inboard gun bay door are illustrated here. This is the door on the left wing, but the one on the right wing would be the same.

There was an internal fuel tank located inside the inboard section of each wing. These two fuel tanks met at the aircraft's centerline under the cockpit. A fueling point was located on top of each wing for these tanks. (USAFM)

Above: The entire left aileron and trim tab are visible in this photograph. The two aerodynamic fairings ahead of the trim tab can also be seen. These fairings were added during the early production of P-51Bs and P-51Cs, and they continued on the P-51Ds and -Ks.

Right. An underside view of the same aileron shows the single fairing on the bottom of the wing.

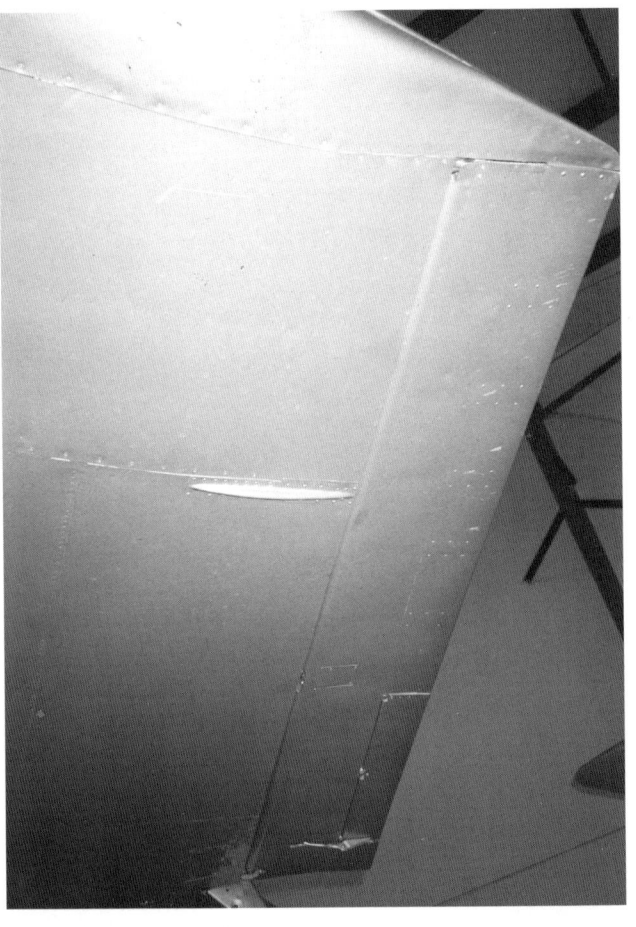

The entire right flap is shown in the photograph at left, while at right is a close-up of the area where the inboard edge of the flap meets the fuselage.

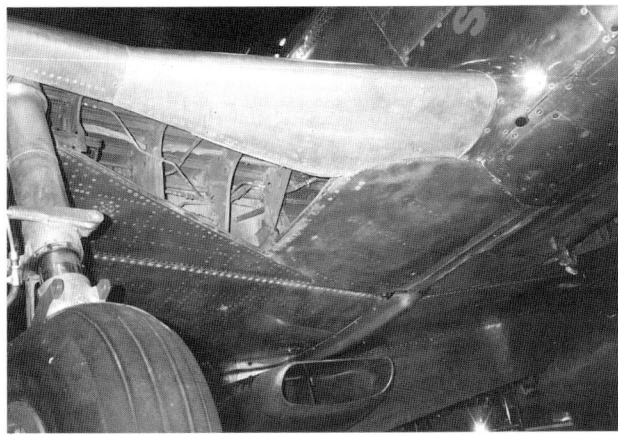

The leading edge of the wing from the landing gear strut to the root was changed from the design used on earlier Mustangs. On the P-51D and -K, a fillet was added which increased the chord of the wing at this point. It also resulted in a much more noticeable change in the direction of the leading edge than had been seen on the earlier versions. This is the fillet on the right wing as viewed from below. Also note the closed inner landing gear doors in this photo.

An overall view of the left flap is provided in this photograph.

Markings on the left flap can be seen here. The red L-shaped marking is a warning to personnel not to step on that area of the flap. The marking that looks like piano keys indicates the extent to which the flap is lowered.

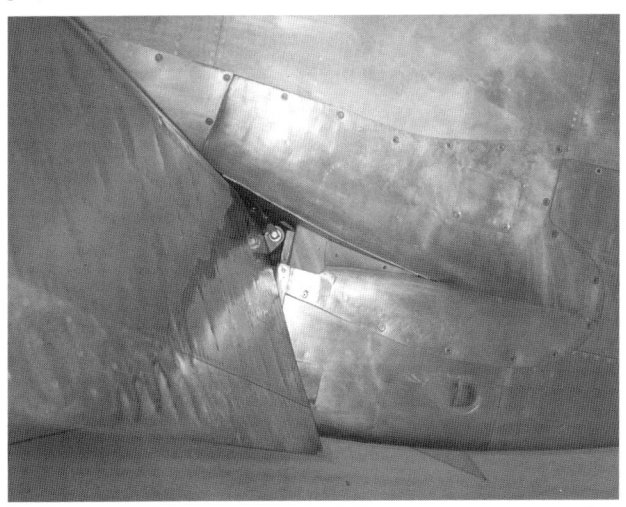

A close-up provides a look at the point where the left flap meets the fuselage.

As with some earlier versions of the Mustang, three identification lights were located under the right wing near the tip.

Mustang variants prior to the P-51D had position lights located on the top and bottom of each wing near the tip. However, on the P-51D and P-51K a single light was mounted right on the wing tip. This photograph also reveals the laminar flow airfoil to good effect.

FUSELAGE DETAILS

The carburetor scoop moved from the top of the nose to a location under the spinner when the Merlin engine replaced the Allison on the P-51B and -C. It remained the same on the P-51D and -K.

On each side of the lower nose section was a perforated inspection panel for the air filter. A non-perforated plate was used on a few aircraft. This is the plate on the left side.

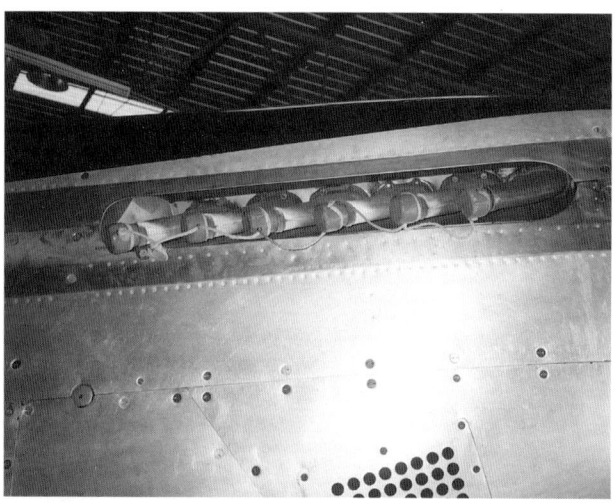

Some P-51Ds and -Ks had unshrouded exhausts as seen in the photograph at left. But most had the shrouded exhausts as illustrated at right.

The port for the flare pistol was located just below the canopy rail on the left side of the fuselage.

Just below the aft end of the canopy on the left side of the fuselage was the filler cap for the fuselage fuel tank. Just aft of it was a grounding point. The filler cap was usually painted red, while the ground point was black with yellow or white lettering.

On the spine of the aircraft, just aft of the canopy, was the slot for the rear canopy guide.

The cooling-air intake was the same configuration and in the same location as it had been on the P-51B and -C.

This photograph looks up inside the hot air exhaust and reveals the aft end of the radiator.

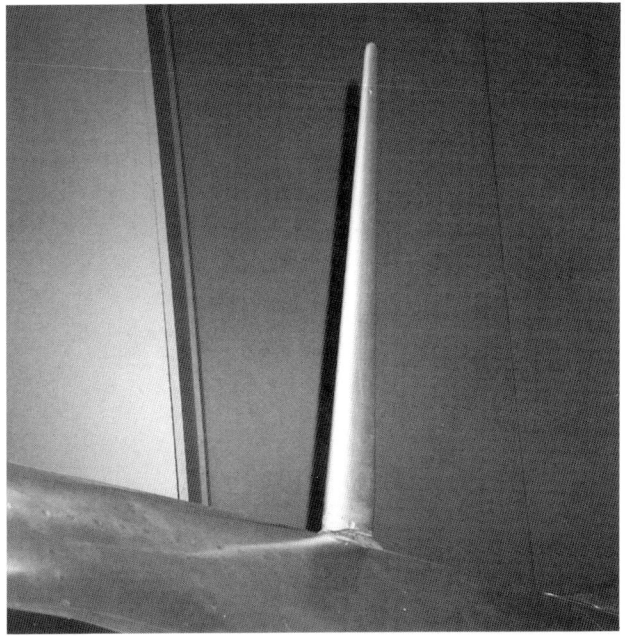

A single radio antenna mast was positioned further aft on the canopy. It was associated with the AN/ARC-3 radio set. On some aircraft this was replaced with a loop antenna, and on others, both the mast and the loop were fitted. Two masts, mounted side by side, were also used late in the Mustang's service life. However, this arrangement was more common on the later P-51H.

The fronts of the radiators can be seen in this view inside the cooling-air scoop.

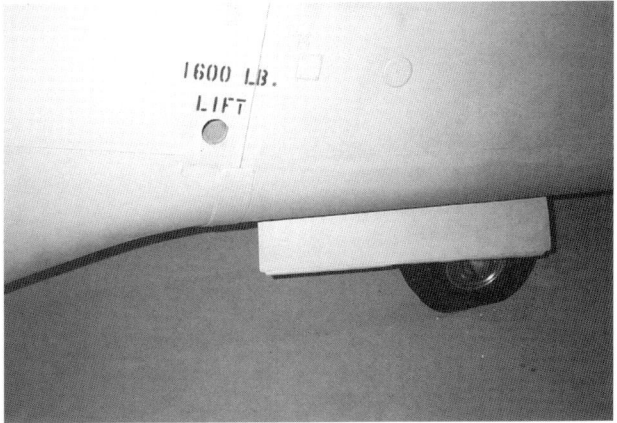

A tube ran laterally all the way through the aft fuselage. A bar could be placed inside the tube, and it was used for hoisting the aft end of the aircraft.

TAIL DETAILS

The antenna wire was attached to the vertical tail just below the fin cap. It ran through the canopy and attached to the back of the pilot's seat. Another wire attached it to the radios located behind the seat.

The AN/APS-13 tail warning radar was added beginning with the P-51D-20-NA and the P-51K-10-NT. It was also retrofitted to some earlier P-51Ds and -Ks. It was also installed on some P-51Hs.

The trim tab on the rudder was controlled by an adjustment arm on the right side of the rudder. It was located at the bottom of the trim tab. The rudder was made of aluminum alloy framework which was covered with doped fabric.

The clear or white tail position light was mounted at the base of the trailing edge of the rudder.

An overall view of the right elevator also shows the counterbalance to good effect. When production of the P-51D and P-51K began, both the elevators and rudder were fabric covered. But these were replaced by metal covered elevators during production of the P-51D-20-NA and P-51K-10-NT. Previous P-51Ds were also retrofitted with metal elevators.

Although not originally on P-51Ds and -Ks, a dorsal fin was added to increase lateral stability.

The left vertical stabilizer and elevator is shown here.

The adjustment arm on the left elevator trim tab was located on the underside.

On the right elevator, the adjustment arm was on the top.

CANOPY DETAILS

There were two slightly different canopies associated with the P-51D and P-51K. One, which had a continuous and even curve to the top of the bubble, is usually thought of as belonging to the P-51D, while the one with a slightly higher profile and an increase in the amount of curvature at the aft end is generally connected to the P-51K. But the fact is that both would fit either version, and in the field, these canopies were often changed between aircraft. So it was common to see both Mustang variants with either type of canopy. This is illustrated in the two photographs above. The same aircraft, P-51D-30-NA, 44-74873, is shown in both photos at different points in time. In the picture at left, it has the canopy usually associated with the P-51K. At right, it is seen with the canopy usually connected to the P-51D. As will be illustrated later in this book, F-82s were sometimes seen with one canopy of each type. In these two photos, the change of markings is also interesting. At left is the original PF prefix to the buzz number, while at right, the subsequent FF prefix is used. Also note the addition of colorful markings to the nose, canopy rail, and tip of the tail.
(Both USAFM)

The button at the bottom of the windscreen releases the canopy and allows it to move backward. A crank just inside the canopy on the right side of the cockpit could then be used to move the canopy aft. The bar just forward of the button was for emergency use only, and completely released the canopy from the aircraft. What appears to be a light colored bar on the canopy rail is actually a yellow handle that can be used to pull the canopy to a closed position.

This right rear view of the canopy reveals the curved interior bracing with lightening holes. Note also the roller on the top of the canopy where the antenna wire passes through it. (Slatton)

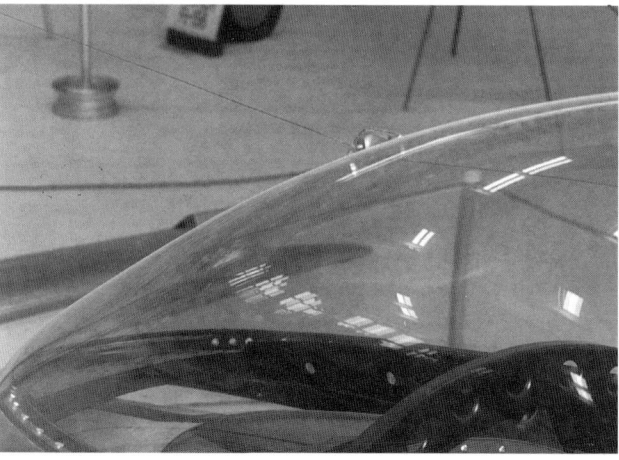

The roller for the antenna wire is shown here again from a different angle.

TP-51D & TF-51D

Ten TP-51Ds were converted from P-51D-25-NTs during 1944. Fifteen more TF-51Ds were modified by Temco in 1951. These were also based on block -25-NT aircraft. Note the lack of doors for the tail wheel. This was because the tail wheel was not retractable on these two-seat Mustangs. (USAFM)

This top view shows the longer rail on the spine for the aft canopy guide. (Slatton)

A longer bubble canopy covered the two cockpits of the TP and TF-51Ds. (Slatton)

The wire antenna could no longer run through the canopy on the two-seat Mustangs. Instead, it was moved to the right side of the fuselage.

EXPERIMENTAL MUSTANGS
XP-51F, XP-51G, & XP-51J

Three lightweight XP-51Fs were built. Although this version used the same Merlin V-1650-7 as the P-51D, it was over 2,500 pounds lighter. As a result, speed was increased by twenty-nine miles per hour. (USAFM)

Another lightweight experiment was the XP-51G. Only two of this type were built, and these were fitted with the Rolls-Royce 145 Merlin which produced 1,500 horsepower. Its maximum take-off weight was less than 9,000 pounds. Although it looks shorter, the XP-51G was the same length as the P-51D and P-51K. (USAFM)

Last of the lightweight Mustang experiments was the XP-51J. It was fitted with the Allison V-1710-119 engine which produced 1,500 horsepower. Only two were built. (USAFM)

P-51H

The P-51H reflected many major design changes when compared to the P-51D and -K. It was more than fifty miles-per-hour faster than the -D and over five hundred pounds lighter. (USAFM)

The P-51H, which first flew on February 3, 1945, may appear to be nearly identical to the previous P-51D. However, the fuselage, wing, and tail section were all redesigned. Even the main landing gear was changed from that on all previous Mustangs. This redesign was accomplished in order to correct some balance problems as well as to lighten the airframe and thereby improve performance. Both empty and gross weights of the P-51H were five-hundred pounds lighter than the P-51D, and maximum speed increased between fifty and eighty-six miles-per-hour depending on altitude and the configuration of the aircraft. The lines of the P-51H were cleaner, and even the exhaust shroud was more streamlined in order to reduce drag.

The P-51H is often called the "tall tail" Mustang, because its vertical tail was noticeably taller than that of all other variants. However, the P-51H-1-NA production block aircraft were all built with a short vertical stabilizer. The change to the tall tail was made during P-51H-5-NA production, and it was accomplished by the addition of a higher fin cap. The height of the rudder was not increased.

The Packard Merlin V-1650-9 engine was equipped with water injection to provide in excess of 2,000 horsepower in a wartime emergency. The standard dry rating was 1,380 horsepower. The engine turned an Aeroproducts A-542-B1 or B2 uncuffed propeller which was 11'1" in diameter.

With a top speed of 487 miles-per-hour in a clean configuration, the P-51H was the fastest propeller-driven aircraft produced during World War II. However, production was so late that the war ended before any of these

Although the P-51H is usually associated with having a tall vertical stabilizer, the early examples had the shorter tail seen here on the fifth P-51H-1-NA. (Both USAFM)

This P-51H was assigned to the 56th Fighter Group at Selfridge Field, Michigan.   (USAFM)

"Hot Rod" Mustangs saw combat service. At the end of the war, defense orders were cut across the board, and the P-51H was no exception. The initial order of 2,000 aircraft was cut to just 555 examples, all of which were built in California. None of these were fitted with cameras for the tactical reconnaissance mission as had been the case for most previous Mustang variants.

It was originally intended that the Dallas plant also build the P-51H under the P-51L designation, but this order was cancelled as well. A P-51M version was also planned for production in Dallas. It was similar to the P-51H except that it was equipped with the V-1650-9A engine which did not have water injection. Only one of these was completed before the remainder of the order was cancelled.

In addition to being faster in the air, improvements were made to make the P-51H easier and faster to maintain on the ground. The internal armament of six .50-caliber machine guns was retained, but the ammunition was loaded in removable boxes that made rearming the weapons much simpler and quicker. Like the late production P-51Ds and P-51Ks, the P-51H could also be fitted with six 5-inch HVAR rockets under its wings. Two bombs could be carried in place of external fuel tanks, and each could be up to the 1,000-pound size.

It has been reported elsewhere that the P-51H was the only single-seat version of the Mustang not to be exported. However, it shares this distinction with the A-36. As with the A-36, one P-51H was turned over to the Royal Air Force for evaluation, however, the British did not place any orders for this version.

As World War II ended, the P-51H began replacing P-51Ds in regular Air Force squadrons, and the older versions were passed on to the Air National Guard, bulldozed into the ground, or cut up and burned without ever returning back to the United States at war's end.

As excellent as the performance of the P-51H was, its days of service with the regular Air Force was limited as the F-80s, F-84s, and F-86 jet fighters began to take their place on the flight lines. The P-51H followed the P-51Ds into the Guard units but were retained there for even a shorter time than many of the older versions. In 1948, all H-models still in service were redesignated F-51H.

"IRON CHIT BIRD" was a P-51H-5-NA. It is shown here on 2 March, 1950, while assigned to the Ohio Air National Guard.   (Menard)

Coverage of the P-51H continues on page 41.

COLOR GALLERY

"Muddy" was a P-51K flown by Jim Gasser of the 362nd Fighter Squadron of the 357th Fighter Group. The name was derived from Gasser's nickname for his mother. Note the AN/APS-13 tail warning antenna on the side of the vertical tail. In the background is "BUTCH BABY," a P-51D which is illustrated on the front cover of this book.
(Sloan via Kuhnert and Ethell)

Thomas P. Smith flew "Caroline," a P-51D assigned to the 370th Fighter Squadron of the 359th Fighter Group. Two kill markings are painted on the canopy rail. (Smith via Ethell)

P-51Ds of the 55th Fighter Group are lined up at Wormingford, England. Aircraft in the front row are coded CY and belong to the 343rd Fighter Squadron. The Mustangs in the second row carry the CL code of the 388th Fighter Squadron, and in the back row are P-51Ds of the 38th Fighter Squadron. The 38th FS used CG fuselage codes. (Ethell collection)

Robert Estrella flew this P-51D with the 83rd Fighter Squadron of the 78th Fighter Group. Note the thin red outline around the fuselage codes as well as the larger red outline on the white rudder. This aircraft does not have the usual black identification bands painted around the wings and horizontal tails. There is one red kill marking on the canopy rail. (Estrella via Ethell)

This F-51H wears the markings of the Arizona Air National Guard. Other than the stencilling on the side of the fuselage, the only unit markings are the yellow tips on the wings, horizontal tails, and fin. Each is outlined in black.   (Hess via Ethell)

This F-51D was assigned to the 12th Fighter Bomber Squadron, and it is shown here in Korea. In 1948, the prefix letters for the buzz numbers on single-engine Mustangs were changed from PF to FF.   (Spry via Ethell)

The Republic of Korea Air Force also operated F-51Ds during the war. This one, and another directly behind it, share the dirt apron at a South Korean airfield with USAF A-26C Invaders.   (Detail & Scale collection)

MERLIN ENGINE DETAILS & COLORS

These two photographs show details of the Merlin engine and its accessories from the left side. Most color photographs of P-51Ds taken during World War II show that the supporting framework for the engine and the covering panels were most often painted Chromate Yellow primer as shown here. However, Chromate Green primer was sometimes used as well. This is a restored P-51D, but it has been rebuilt exactly to factory specifications for late production P-51Ds including the colors used for the paints and primers. (Both Slatton)

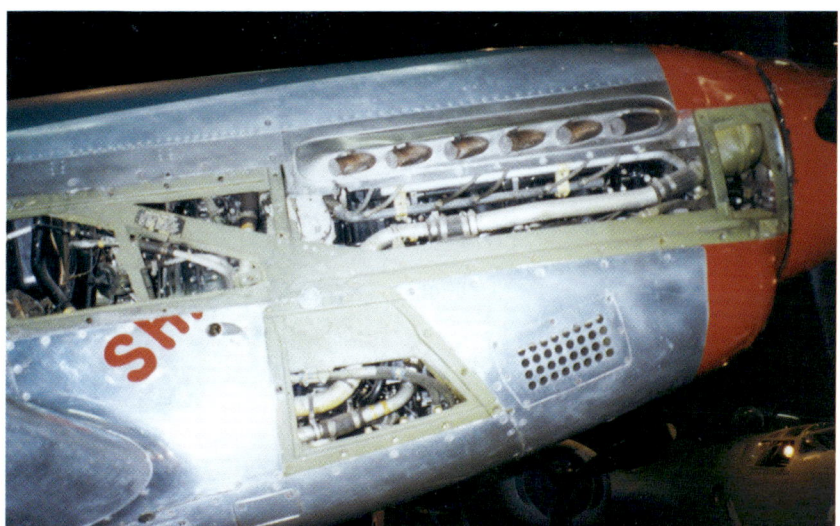

This F-51D was turned over to the USAF Museum from the West Virginia Air National Guard. Chromate Green primer can be seen on the framework of this aircraft. While color photographs taken of Mustangs in the field show that Chromate Green primer was sometimes used on these areas, it appears to have been far less common than the Chromate Yellow primer.

The engine installation in a P-51H is illustrated in these two views. A study of similarities and differences between the P-51H and the P-51D can be made by comparing these two photographs with the three above. Note particularly the differences in the framework that supports the engine, necessitated by the redesign of the fuselage. The shape of the exhaust ports is illustrated in the photograph at right. (Both Reoder)

P-51D COCKPIT DETAILS & COLORS

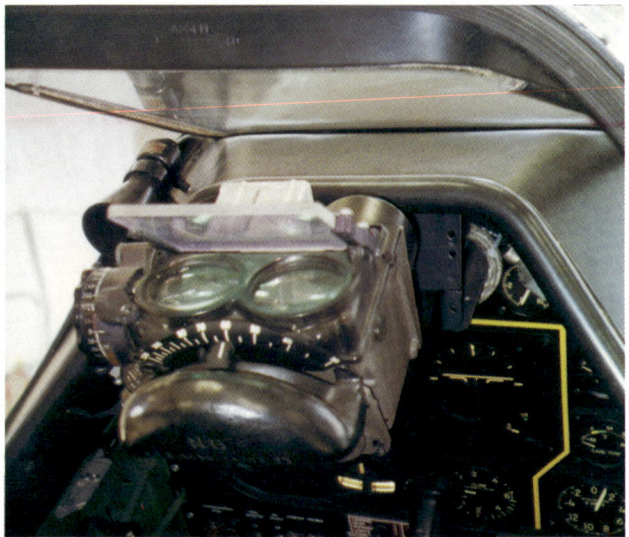

The photographs on this page and the next were taken in a P-51D which has been restored to factory standards as specified for a late production P-51D. The only difference is that the floor is a higher grade of plywood than called for in the specifications. These two views show details of the K-14B gyro-computing gunsight from different angles. This gunsight was an improvement over the reflector sights used in earlier Mustangs.

The instrument panel changed very little from one Mustang variant to another until the introduction of the P-51H.

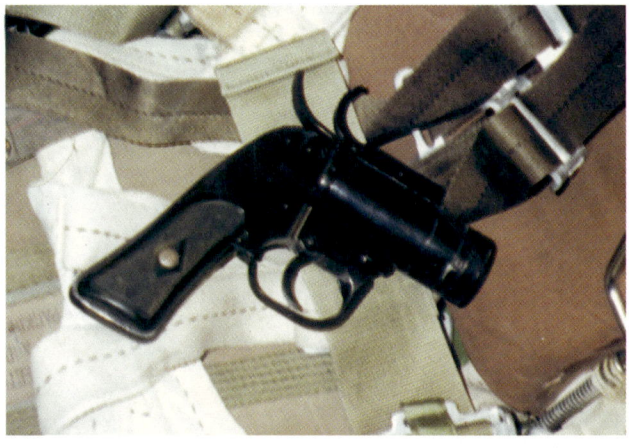

A flare pistol was carried inside the cockpit. It could be fired through a port in the left side of the fuselage.

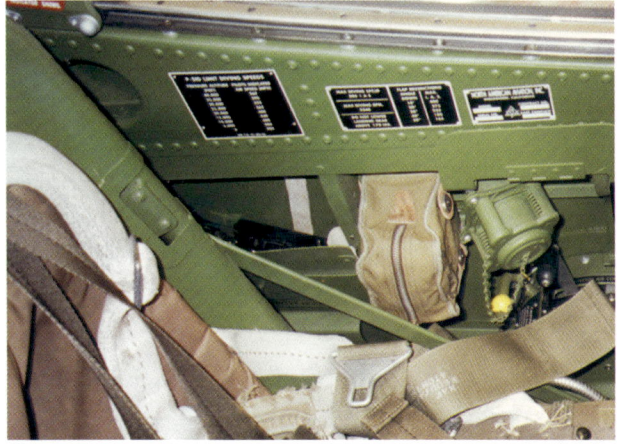

The port through which the flare pistol was fired can be seen mounted at a slight angle just above the belt in this close-up. Note the three placards on the side of the fuselage. The aft two relate to diving speeds and the use of flaps, while the forward one is the manufacturer's placard concerning the production of the aircraft.

An overall view of the left side of the cockpit is provided here. Note the throttle quadrant and trim wheels. The two horizontal wheels are for the rudder and aileron trim, while the vertical one is the elevator trim wheel.

The control column and the lower part of the instrument panel can be seen in this view. Note the Chromate Yellow primer which shows through the cutout in the center of the plywood floor. This is actually the top of the center wing section which is only a few inches below the floor.

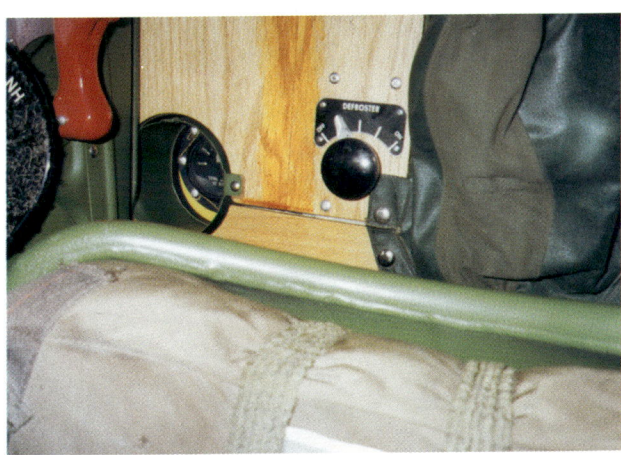

This is the left rear corner of the cockpit floor. The gage in the floor, which is just forward of the seat, is the fuel quantity gage for the left wing tank. The gage is mounted on the metal wing structure, and is visible through a hole in the wooden floor. A similar gage is on the right side of the cockpit floor for the right wing tank. Also visible is a selector knob for the defroster air. Another knob, located in a similar position on the right side of the floor, is the control for hot air. (Slatton)

Details of the right rudder pedal can be seen here. The left pedal was the same. Note the North American Aviation logo at the top of the pedal.

The right side of the cockpit was occupied mostly by radio equipment. This varied from aircraft to aircraft and from time period to time period. This aircraft has the AN/APS-13 tail warning radar panel located just under the canopy crank. Engine operating limitations are on the large center placard on this side of the cockpit.

The headrest and armor plate behind the pilot's seat can be seen here.

P-51D GUN BAY DETAILS & COLORS

Three .50-caliber machine guns were mounted in each wing of the P-51D. This was a fifty percent increase over the firepower available in the P-51A, P-51B, and P-51C. After the tilted guns in earlier Mustangs experienced jamming problems, the guns in the P-51D were mounted upright. According to USAAF specifications, the interior of the bays were painted Chromate Yellow primer. However, color photographs show that Chromate Green primer was also used, particularly in the post-war period. This is the gun bay in the left wing as seen from behind.

A placard was mounted inside the forward cover for each gun bay. At the top was information for bore sighting the guns, while in the center were instructions for loading the ammunition. At the bottom were special instructions for oiling the guns and using the gun heaters.

The gun bay in the right wing is shown here. The view looks outboard in the bay, and the ammunition feed chutes are clearly visible.

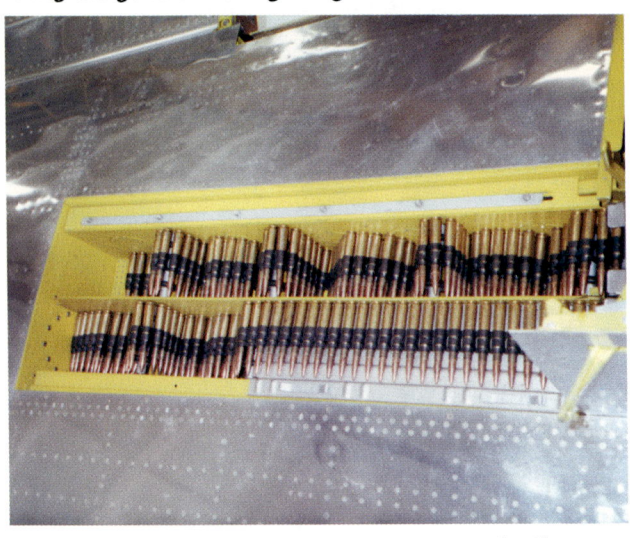

This is the ammunition pile up or storage area for the guns in the right wing.

These two views show both gun bays looking aft. At left is the gun bay in the right wing, and at right is the bay in the left wing.

P/F-82 TWIN MUSTANG COLORS

Arctic markings adorn this natural metal F-82G of the 449th FIS. This unit was stationed at Elmendorf AFB, Alaska.   (Spry via Ethell)

Above: Col. Oliver Cellini's F-82F is shown here in the markings of the 52nd All Weather Group at Mitchell Air Force Base. Col. Cellini was the unit's commanding officer.
(Larkins via Spry and Ethell)

Right: "SIAMESE LADY" was an F-82F assigned to the 68th F(AW)S at Suwon Air Base, Korea, in 1951.
(Filer via Olmstead and Ethell)

P/F-82B COCKPIT DETAILS & COLORS

At left is the left cockpit in "Betty Jo," the P/F-82B which set the distance record flying non-stop and unrefueled from Hawaii to New York. At right is the right cockpit. Although a couple of instruments have been removed, and there has been some deterioration of the right cockpit, the two cockpits remain very much as they were fifty years ago when the aircraft was in service. Note the floor in each of the cockpits.

The sides were very much the same in both cockpits of the P/F-82B. This is the left side of the pilot's cockpit.

Details on the right side of the co-pilot's cockpit can be seen in this photograph.

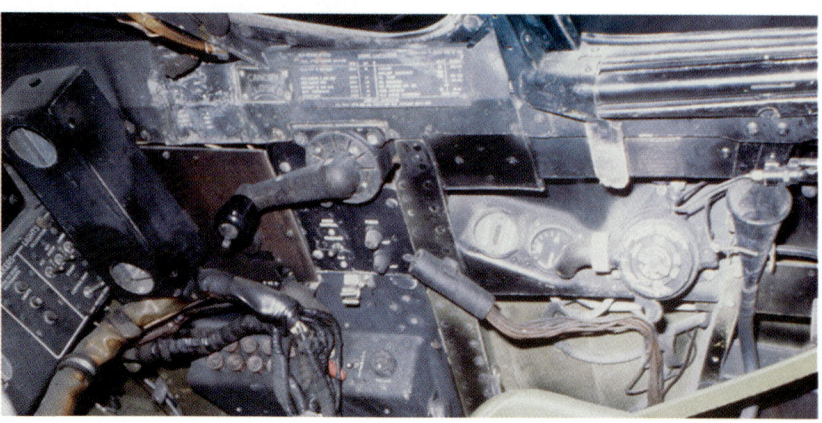

AIR NATIONAL GUARD P-51Hs

As jets became available to the U. S. Air Force, P-51Hs were quickly turned over to units of the Air National Guard. Eight states are represented in the photographs on this page. At left is an aircraft from the New Jersey Guard, while at right is a P-51H from the New Hampshire Guard. Note the loop antenna behind the pilot's seat on these and several other aircraft on this page. (Both USAFM)

The states of Maine and Maryland are represented by these two Mustangs. The twin antenna masts are clearly visible on the aircraft at right. (Both USAFM)

Guard units from Ohio and Illinois also flew P-51Hs. These two photographs illustrate that, like the P-51D and P-51K, the P-51H used both styles of canopies. (Both USAFM)

The P-51H shown at left is painted in silver dope and is from the California Air Guard. At right is a natural metal aircraft with the colorful markings used by the Texas Air National Guard. (Both USAFM)

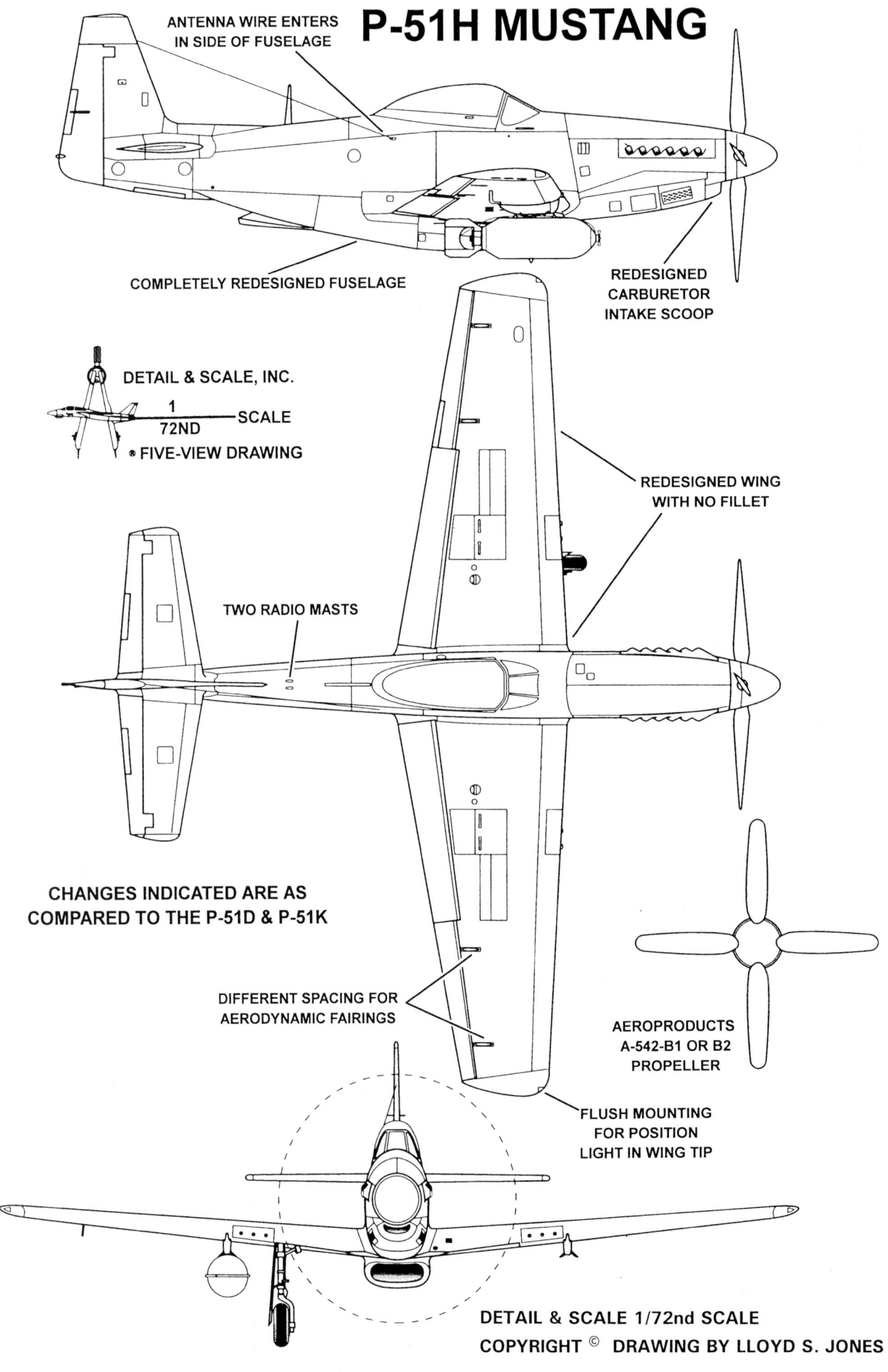

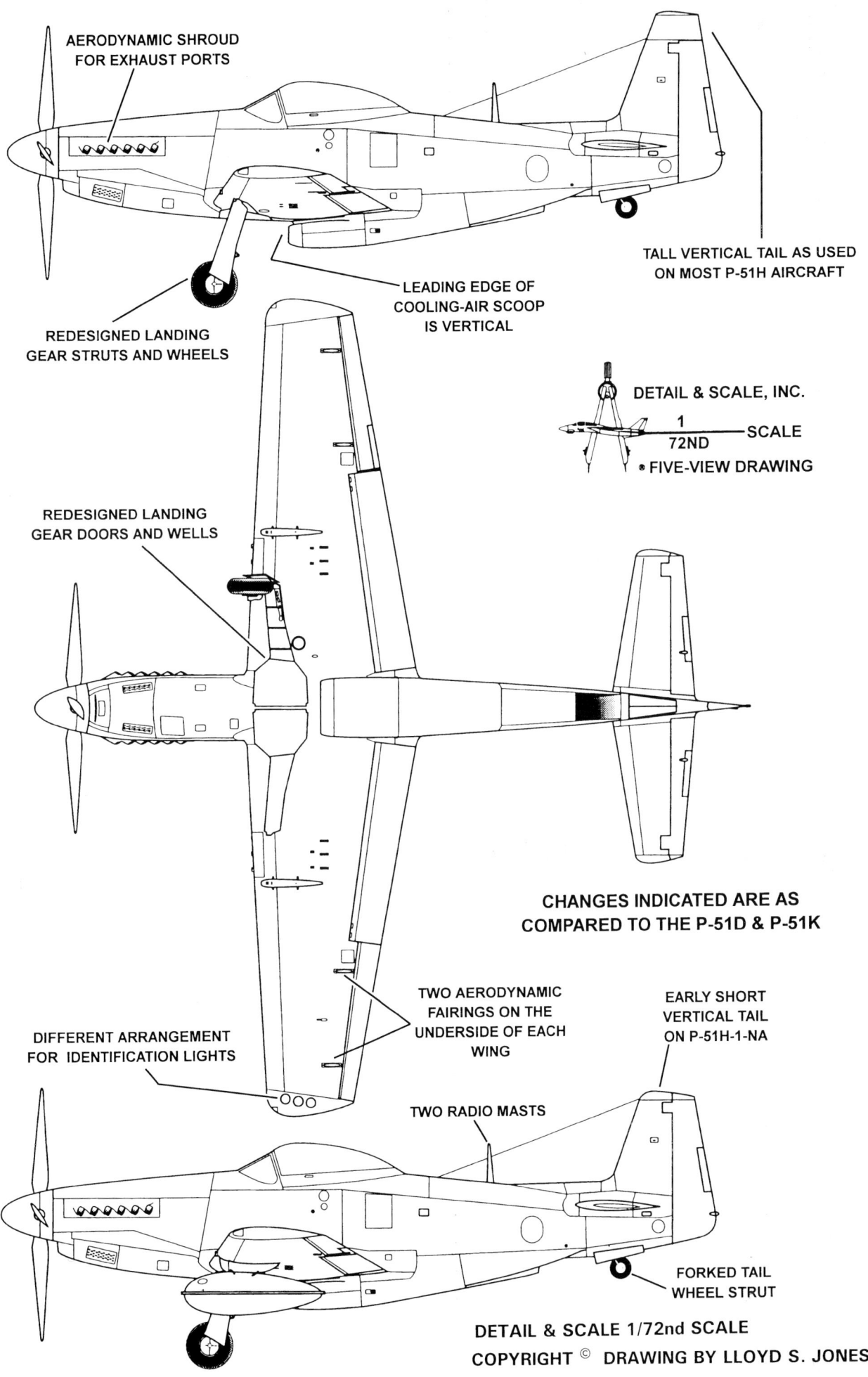

P-51H DETAIL DIFFERENCES

The photographs on this page and the next three illustrate the major physical differences between the P-51H and the previous P-51D. The propeller was changed to the Aeroproducts four-blade A-542B1 or B2. It was uncuffed and was 11'1" in diameter. (Roeder)

The entire wing was redesigned, and the leading edge was straight all the way to the fuselage. There was no fillet as there had been on the P-51D and -K. (Roeder)

The exhausts were covered by a streamlined shroud. The natural metal shroud can be seen here on one of the removed engine panels. This is the panel for the left side of the engine compartment. (Roeder)

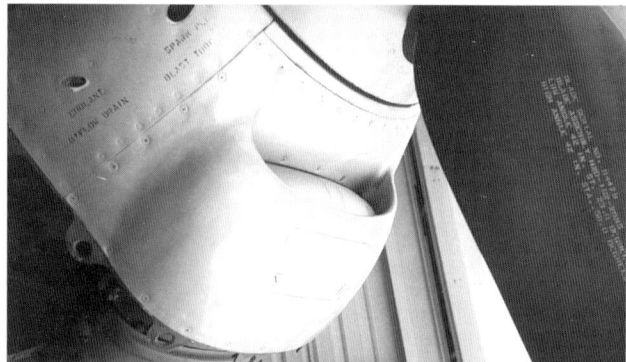

The carburetor intake was in the same location as on the P-51D and -K, but it was of a slightly different design. (Roeder)

Details of the tall tail can be seen here. Note that the rudder extends upward only a couple of inches higher than the counterbalance. (Roeder)

The navigation lights on the wing tips were changed from the teardrop-shaped design to this flush-mounted light on the leading edge of the wing tip. (Roeder)

The landing/taxi lights that hung down from the wheel wells on the P-51D/-K were eliminated and replaced with a single unit just aft of the left wheel well. It retracted flush with the wing when not in use. (Roeder)

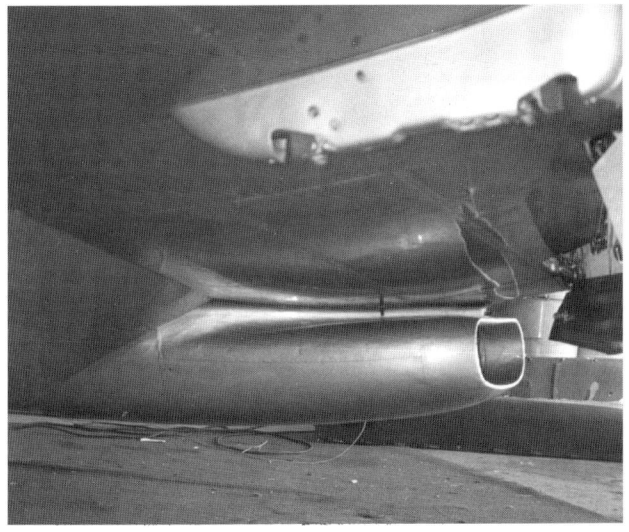

The cooling-air scoop was also redesigned. It was not as wide, and the lip was vertical rather than being at a slant. (Both Roeder)

The tail wheel was mounted on a fork that attached to both sides of the wheel rather than being on only one side as on the earlier variants. The doors were vertical when in the open position. In this case, the aircraft has been pushed back into its parked position, so the wheel has castored around. (Both Roeder)

The main gear was quite different from that used on previous Mustangs. This is the right main gear as viewed from the front and slightly to the inside. Note the retraction strut. This was not on the earlier variants. (Roeder)

Right: The shape of the inner main gear door was completely changed on the P-51H. (Roeder)

The design of the outer door and the wheel hubs also was completely different. The door was almost rectangular in shape and was much thinner than on previous Mustangs. The white blade antenna in the background was added to this restored aircraft and was not present on vintage P-51Hs. (Roeder)

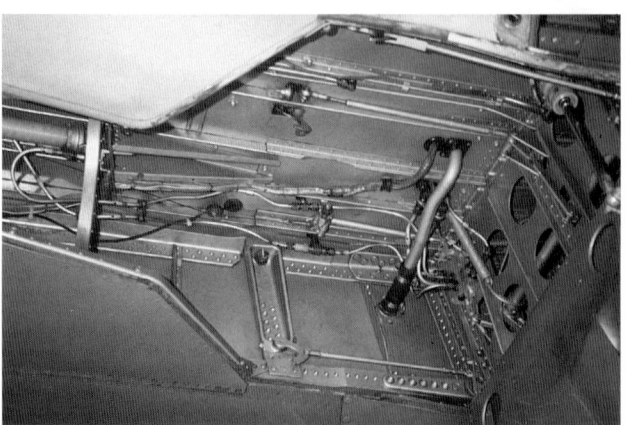

These two views show details inside the right main gear well. It was changed considerably from that used on any of the previous Mustangs. Note that the retraction actuator for the inner door has been moved back to the front of the door. It can be seen near the top right corner of the photograph at right. The actuator had been in this location up through the P-51B and -C, then moved to the aft end of the door and well for the P-51D and -K. (Both Roeder)

P-51H COCKPIT DETAILS

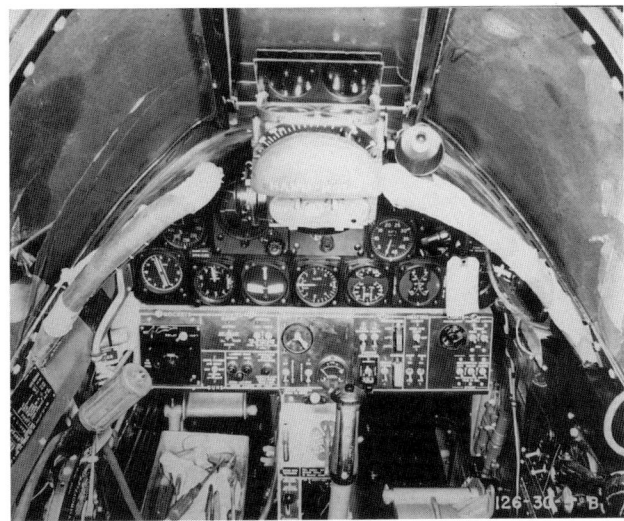

All versions of the Mustang up through the P-51D/-K had cockpit layouts that were very similar. But in the P-51H, the features of the cockpit were changed considerably. This is the instrument panel as used in the P-51H. (NAA via Morgan and Rockwell)

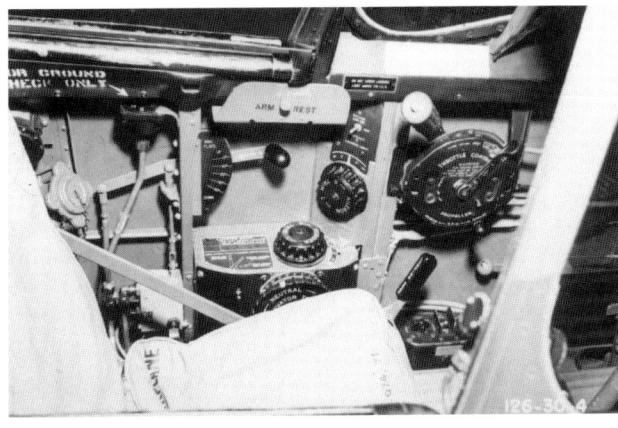

Details on the left side of the cockpit are shown in this photograph. Compare this with the pictures of the P-51D cockpit shown on page 36. Also note the diagonal brace on the seat. (NAA via Morgan and Rockwell)

With the seat removed, details of the right side of the cockpit are easy to see in this photograph. (NAA via Morgan and Rockwell)

The left rudder pedal, the center console located just below the instrument panel, and the control column can be seen here. (NAA via Morgan and Rockwell)

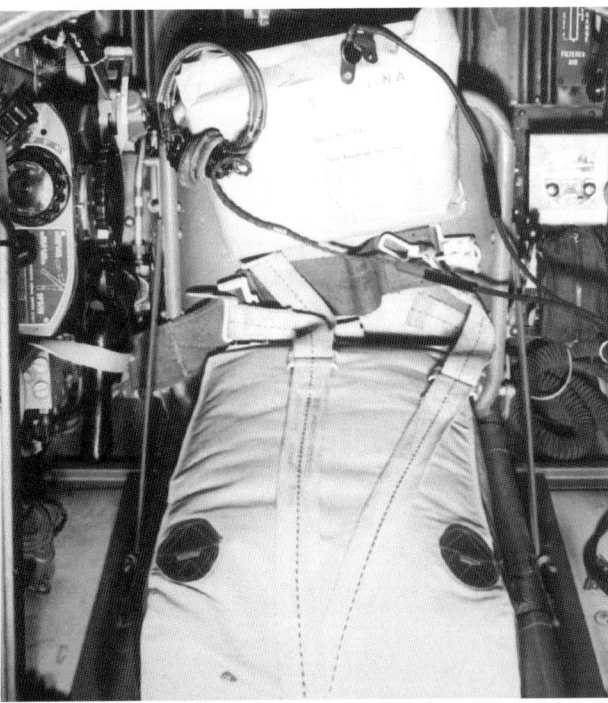

This view looks straight down into the cockpit and shows the seat, harness and belts, and the headphones (NAA via Morgan and Rockwell)

P/F-82 TWIN MUSTANG

The need for a long-range fighter to escort bombers to Japan resulted in the development of the Twin Mustang. It had two fuselages that were similar to that used on the P-51H, but they were lengthened from 33' 4" to 39' 1". This was due mostly to a plug in each fuselage, but the larger vertical tails also contributed to this increase. However, the aircraft was far more involved than simply bolting two Mustangs together. The second of the two XP-82 prototypes is shown here with a standard P-51D in the background. (USAFM)

Warfare against Japan's home islands posed many difficult problems to America's military planners. Invasion of an island nation could only come from the sea, and only after a large scale bombing campaign. Neither the bombers or fighters on hand in 1943 were capable of adequately handling the task, primarily because of the great distances that would have to be flown. The B-29 was developed as the bomber that would meet these needs, but the USAAF wanted a fighter that was capable of escorting it to Japan where it was certain to meet fierce enemy opposition.

In January of 1944, the USAAF ordered four prototypes of the P-82 Twin Mustang. This unusual fighter would have a maximum range of 2,600 miles, which was 300 miles more than the P-51D, and over the Pacific Ocean every mile would be precious. More importantly, the P-82 carried two pilots who could relieve each other during missions that might last as long as nine hours. But it is interesting to note that only the pilot in the left fuselage had full IFR instruments. On such missions in the "soup," the second pilot would be able to provide little in the way of relief.

North American joined two modified and lengthened P-51H fuselages with constant cord center wing and tail sections. The outer wing panels remained similar to what was on the P-51H, although there were several noticeable differences. The six .50-caliber machine guns were moved to the center wing section to concentrate their fire, and the main landing gear folded into wells under the two fuselages.

Although the order was cut to only two XP-82 prototypes, work continued, and the first flight was made on

This top view of one of the prototypes shows an important feature of the Twin Mustang that has often been misrepresented in drawings. The trailing edge of the wing's center section is further aft than the trailing edge of the root of the two outer sections. (USAFM)

April 15, 1945. It was powered by two Packard Merlin V-1650-23 or -25 engines, and performance was equal to that of a P-51D. Although no P-82As were built, five-hundred P-82Bs were ordered in June 1944, long before either prototype flew. But the end of the war caused production to be cut to only twenty aircraft, and none of these ever saw combat. It is interesting to note that on the P-82B and all subsequent Twin Mustangs, the propeller rotation was changed so that the top tips turned inward toward each other. This was opposite from the rotation used on the XP-82.

The USAAF did see some promise in the design, because a radar observer could replace the second pilot. This made the Twin Mustang a good candidate for all-weather and night operations. Accordingly, the USAAF ordered two of the P-82Bs to be converted to night-fighter prototypes. P-82B-1-NA, 44-65169, became the P-82C, and P-82B-1-NA, 44-65170, became the P-82D. These first flew on 27 and 29 March, 1946, respectively, and they served as developmental aircraft for the later P-82F, P-82G, and P-82H.

Meanwhile, the P-82E was developed as a long-range escort fighter. It was similar to the previous P-82B, but it was powered with Allison 1710-143 or -145 engines. This Allison powerplant would be installed on all subsequent P/F-82 versions. One hundred P-82Es were built, and these became the Strategic Air Command's first long-range escort fighters for the B-29, B-36, and B-50. The 27th Fighter Escort Group (SAC) was the first unit to become operational with any Twin Mustang variant.

The P-82F made its first flight on March 11, 1948, and three months later, the pursuit type was replaced by the fighter type as the U. S. Army Air Forces became the United States Air Force. All aircraft designated previously with a P prefix were changed to an F prefix. Thus, the P-82 became the F-82, and the P-51 became the F-51.

Most F-82s were produced as all-weather night fighters, with the first being the F-82F. This version was equipped with the AN/APG-28 tracking radar, and a total of ninety-one were built. These were followed by forty-five F-82Gs which carried the SCR-720C search radar that had been previously proven in the P-61 Black Widow. In both types, the right cockpit was modified with the necessary controls and displays for operation of the radar. The last nine F-82Fs ordered (44-496 through 44-504) and the last five F-82Gs (44-384 through 44-388) were winterized for service in Alaska and redesignated as F-82Hs.

Although the Twin Mustang's service with the USAF was limited, it did leave some indelible marks on aviation history. A specially modified P-82B named *Betty Jo* establish a non-stop unrefueled distance record by flying from Hickam Field, Hawaii, to Mitchell Field, New York, in 1946. This record still stands today as the greatest distance flown by an unrefueled fighter.

On June 27, 1950, shortly after the beginning of the Korean War, an F-82G from the 68th F(AW)S of the 8th Fighter Bomber Wing shot down a North Korean Yak fighter near Kimpo Air Field north of Seoul. This became the first aerial kill of the war and the first scored by a pilot in the United States Air Force. The F-82G was flown by Lt. William Hudson, and the radar observer was Lt. Carl Fraser. In addition to this first, the Twin Mustang became the last propeller-driven fighter ordered into production by the United States Air Force.

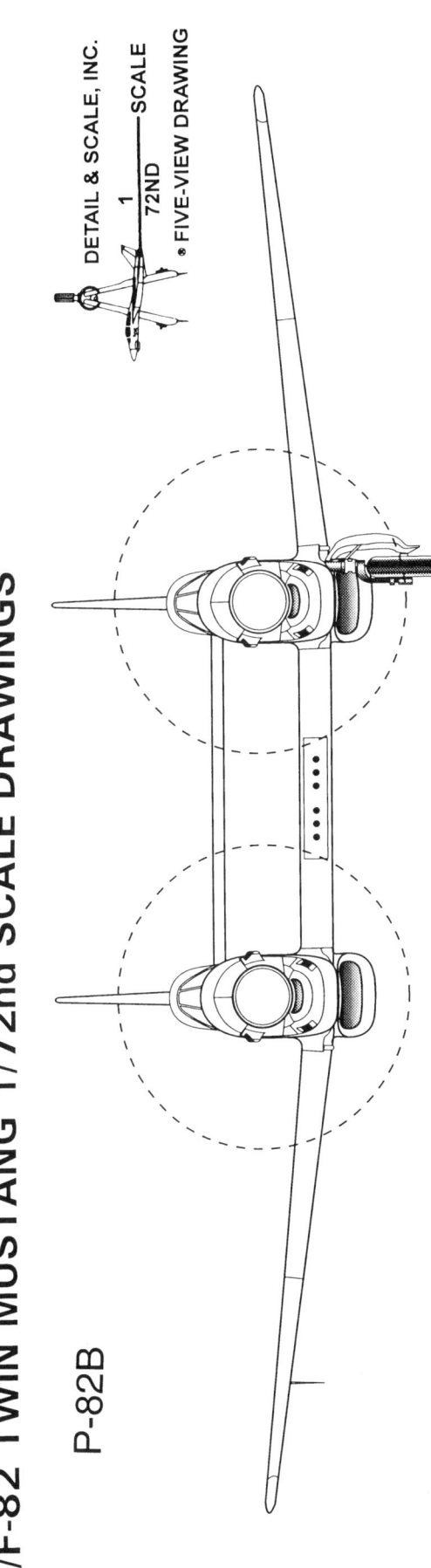

P/F-82 TWIN MUSTANG 1/72nd SCALE DRAWINGS

P-82B

DETAIL & SCALE 1/72nd SCALE COPYRIGHT © DRAWING BY LLOYD S. JONES

P-82B

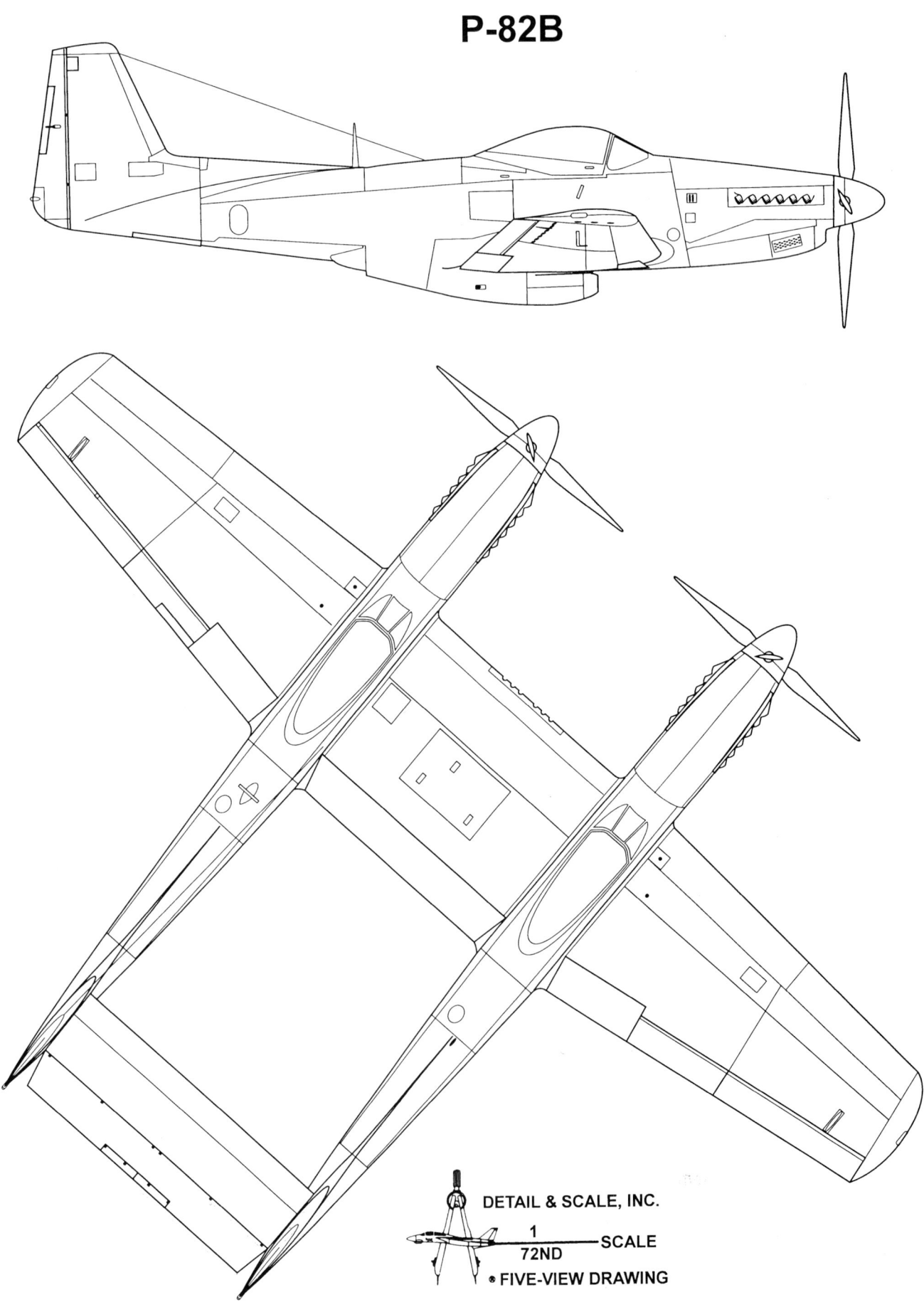

DETAIL & SCALE 1/72nd SCALE COPYRIGHT© DRAWING BY LLOYD S. JONES

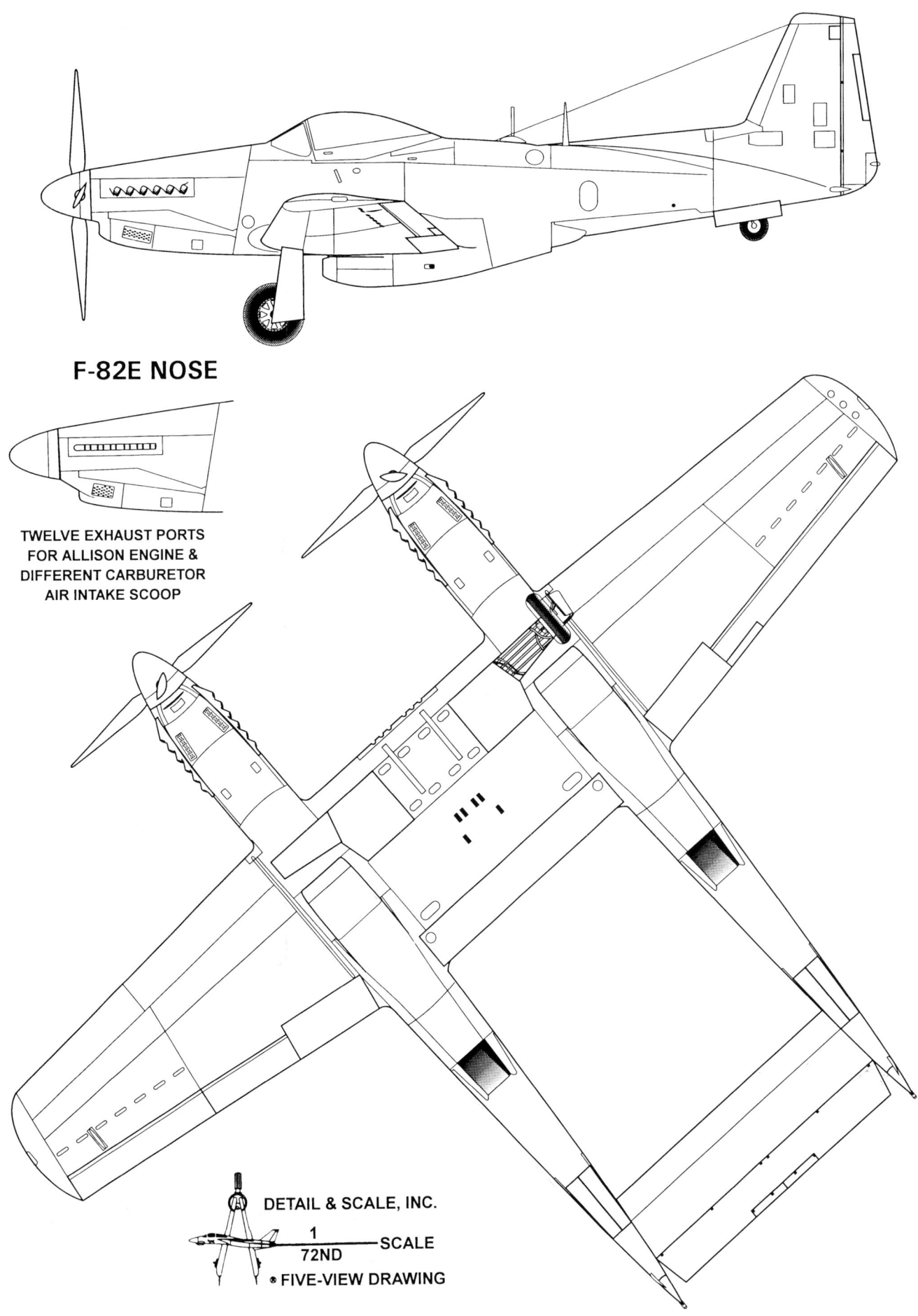

F-82E NOSE

TWELVE EXHAUST PORTS FOR ALLISON ENGINE & DIFFERENT CARBURETOR AIR INTAKE SCOOP

DETAIL & SCALE, INC.
1/72ND SCALE
FIVE-VIEW DRAWING

DETAIL & SCALE 1/72nd SCALE COPYRIGHT © DRAWING BY LLOYD S. JONES

F-82G

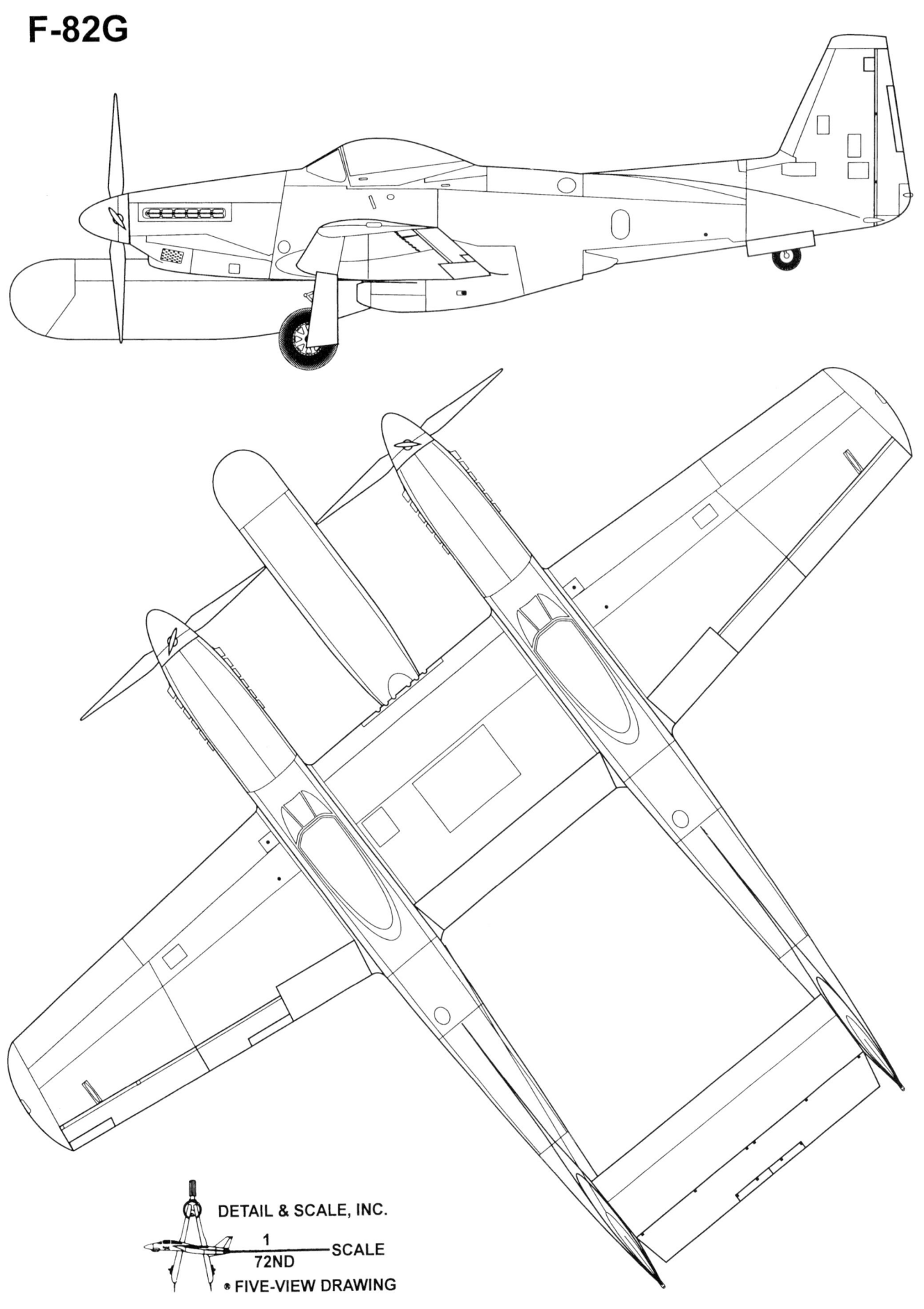

DETAIL & SCALE, INC.
SCALE 1/72ND
FIVE-VIEW DRAWING

DETAIL & SCALE 1/72nd SCALE COPYRIGHT © DRAWING BY LLOYD S. JONES

P/F-82 TWIN MUSTANG DIMENSIONS

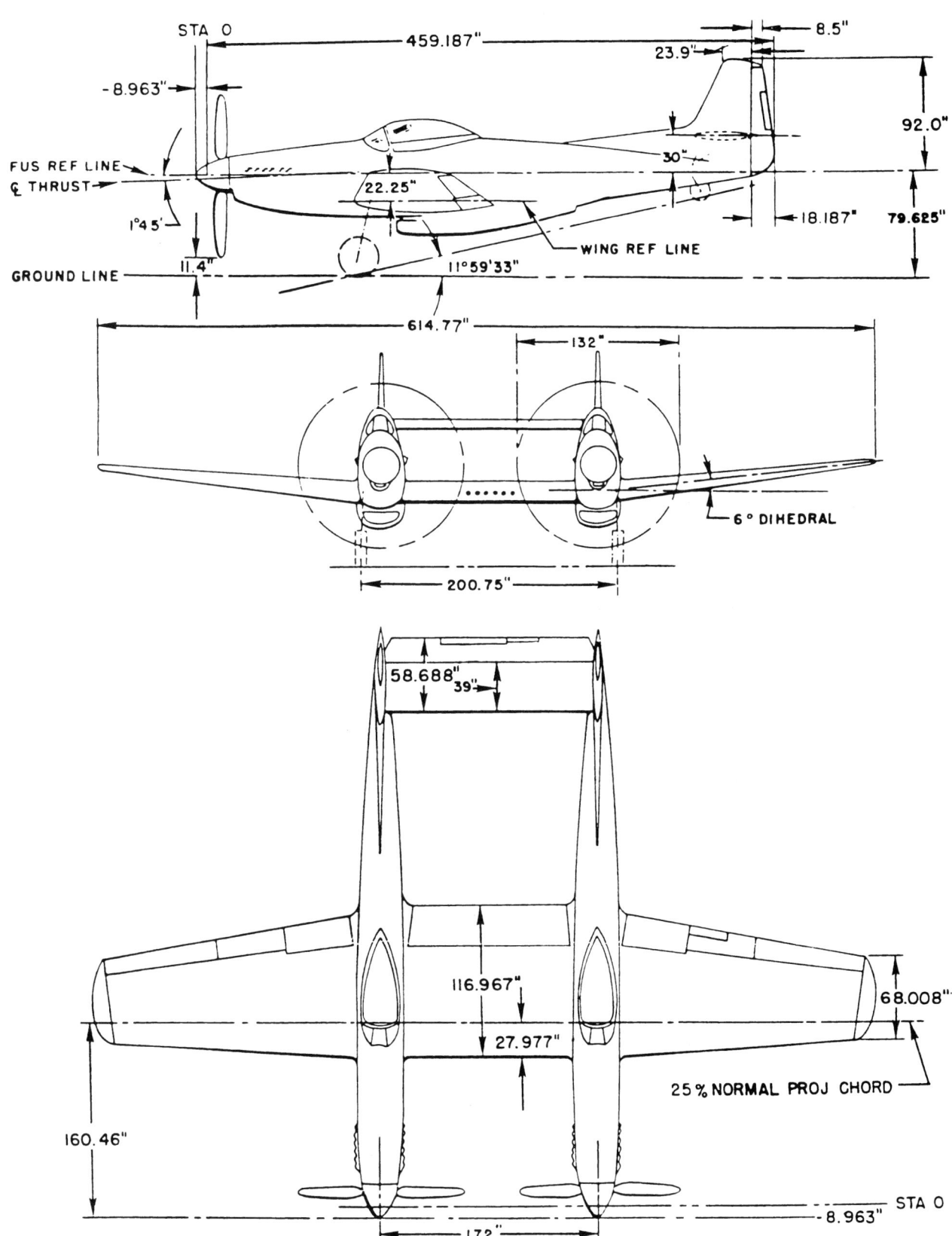

XP-82

Although the Twin Mustang arrived too late to participate in World War II, the large airframe offered considerable possibilities. The end of the war and the jet age caught up with it, so only limited numbers were produced. However, those that were produced did enter service as long-range day fighters and radar-equipped night fighters. *(USAFM)*

When range was not a factor, the powerful Twin Mustang could be turned into what amounted to a flying battleship. In addition to its six internal machine guns, a considerable amount of ordnance could be hung under the large wing. These two photographs, and the two below, show the XP-82 during armament tests with various ordnance combinations. In the photo to the left, the aircraft is fitted with a machine gun pod with eight additional machine guns, ten 5-inch HVAR rockets, and two 500-pound bombs. At right, the machine gun pod has been replaced with two 1000-pound bombs. Also note that the engine on the right fuselage turned its propeller in a clockwise direction as viewed from the cockpit, while the engine in the left fuselage turned its propeller in a counter-clockwise direction. These directions were reversed on production P-82Bs and all subsequent versions. *(Both USAFM)*

The unusual stores combination shown at left consists of ten 5-inch rockets, a 110-gallon fuel tank under the right wing, a 445-gallon fuel tank under the center wing section, and a chemical tank under the left wing. At right is a close-up of the multiple rocket launchers with five rockets on each. *(Both USAFM)*

P/F-82B

Five-hundred P-82Bs were ordered, but only twenty were completed before the remainder of the order was cancelled. This photograph illustrates that the propellers turned in opposite directions than they did on the XP-82 prototype. This is the fourth P-82B built.
(USAFM)

This P-82B is armed with twenty-four 5-inch HVAR rockets which are mounted in pairs. Note the loop antenna behind the left cockpit.
(USAFM)

The most famous P-82B was "Betty Jo." This aircraft set a distance record by flying non-stop and unrefueled from Hickam Field, Hawaii, to Mitchell Field, New York, in fourteen hours and thirty-three minutes. The mission was flown by Lt Col. R. E. Thacker and Lt. J. M. Ard. The flight covered 5,051 miles, not 9,000 miles as reported elsewhere. This aircraft is now on display at the U. S. Air Force Museum.
(USAFM)

P/F-82E

One hundred P-82Es were built, and these were redesignated F-82Es in 1948. As a result, the buzz letters changed from PQ to FQ. This version marked a return to the Allison engine, with the V-1710-143 or -145 being installed. The twelve small exhaust ports on each side of the nose sections were an easy way to distinguish the F-82E from the P/F-82B, which had six ports on each side in a streamlined shroud like the P-51H. (USAFM)

This pod, which could be mounted under the center wing section, carried eight additional .50-caliber machine guns. This raised the firepower of the F-82E to fourteen guns which was considerable by any standard.
(NAA via Jones)

At left is a look inside the gun pod with the front cover removed. The photograph at right shows how the ammunition boxes slid into the pod. (Both NAA via Jones)

NIGHT FIGHTER PROTOTYPES
P-82C & P-82D

P-82B, 44-65169, was converted to the sole P-82C night fighter. It made its first flight on 27 March, 1946, and it served as a prototype for the subsequent F-82F. Red lettering was used on the black finish. Note that both canopy types are fitted to this aircraft. The designation for this aircraft was subsequently changed to ZF-82C in 1948. (USAFM)

The cross section of the SCR-720 radar pod can be seen in this overhead view. (USAFM)

P-82B, 44-65170, was modified to the only P-82D and was fitted with the APS-4 radar pod. This aircraft made its first flight on 29 March, 1946, two days after the P-82C. It was subsequently redesignated EF-82D in 1948. Note that this aircraft retained the Merlin V-1750 engine used in the P-82B, as indicated by the six exhaust ports on each side of the nose.
(NAA via Jones)

The P-82D was fitted with the APS-4 radar, and its small white pod can be seen hanging beneath the center wing section. (NAA via Jones)

NIGHT FIGHTER VERSIONS
F-82F, F-82G, & F-82H

One-hundred F-82F night fighters were built, and nine were winterized for service in Alaska. These were designated F-82Hs. This aircraft was assigned to the 52nd All Weather Fighter Group in 1948. Flash dampeners were installed on the exhausts on the F-82F's Allison V-1710-143 or -145 engines. (USAFM)

The right engine has already started as the pilot and radar observer begin a training flight in FQ-426. Note that there are no antennas on the spines of most night fighter variants. (USAFM)

The flash-dampening exhausts can be seen on this F-82F. Also note the landing/taxi light hanging down under the left wing. The landing gear strut and wheel are flat silver. (USAFM)

The F-82G was also powered by two Allison V-1710-143 or -145 engines. On Twin Mustangs powered by Allison engines, the carburetor scoop was of a different design and was located further aft than the ones on the Merlin powered variants. The scoop used with the Allison powered Twin Mustangs can be seen in this photograph. Five F-82Gs were winterized for use in Alaska as F-82Hs. This particular aircraft was not an F-82H as reported elsewhere. F-82Gs built to F-82H standards were serial numbers 46-384 through 46-388. (USAFM)

P/F-82 DETAILS   LANDING GEAR DETAILS

"Betty Jo," the famous P/F-82B that made the long-distance flight from Hawaii to New York, is now on display at the U. S. Air Force Museum. The photographs on this and the next three pages show details of this well known Twin Mustang. The right main landing gear is seen here from both the inside and the outside. Because the aircraft is on display in a museum, there is no hydraulic fluid in the system. Therefore the oleos on the landing gear are fully compressed. They would be extended several inches under operational conditions.

At left is a front view of the right main landing gear showing the angle of the outer door. Note also the landing/taxi light mounted on the inside of the door. The photo at right shows details of the right main gear well and strut.

Details of the brakes on the left main landing gear are shown here.

The interior of the left gear well is shown in this view.

The unusual shape of the outer gear door can be seen here as can the design of the main gear wheel.

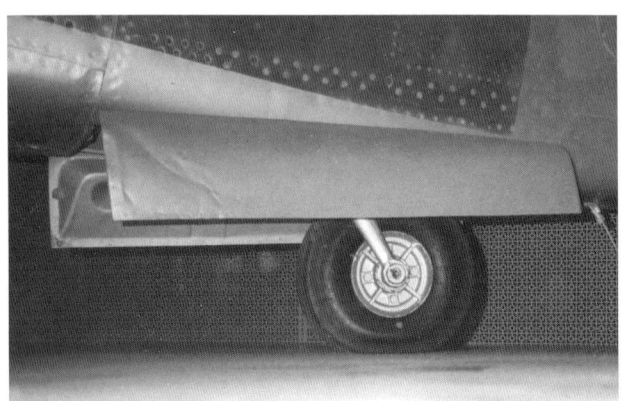

The tail landing gear was the same on both fuselages. At left is the tail wheel on the right fuselage from the inside. At right is a view from the front. Note the retracting rods for the gear doors and the forked strut for the wheel.

WING DETAILS

Above and right: Single aerodynamic fairings were located on both the top and the bottom of each wing just forward of the ailerons. In the photo above, the fairing on the top of the left wing can be seen. At right is the fairing on the underside of the same wing. Also note the series of oval-shaped holes.

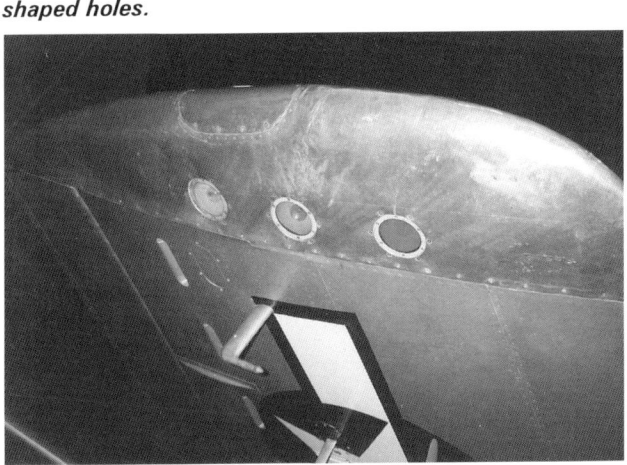

Three identification lights were under the right wing tip. Note also that the F-82 had the L-shaped pitot tube as did all single-seat Mustangs except the A-36. However, it was located much closer to the wing tip. A metal plate on the tip covers where the navigation light used to be.

The area where personnel could step on the trailing edge of the wing root was outlined in red. This was a "no-step" area on single-seat Mustangs.

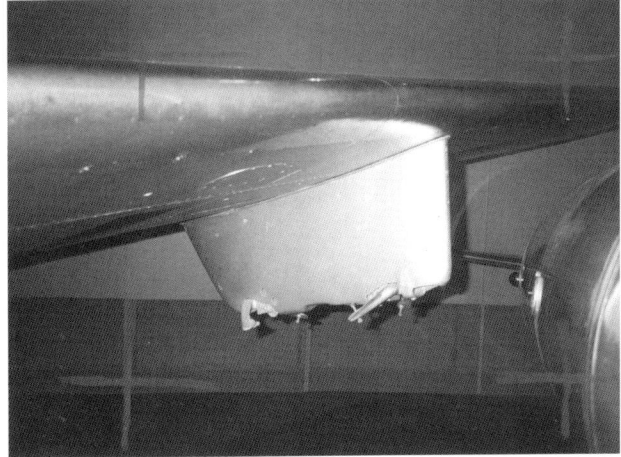

Different types of pylons were used under the outer wing sections on the P/F-82. At left is the smaller pylon that was similar to the ones used on single-seat Mustangs. A much larger pylon is shown at right.

FUSELAGE DETAILS

Aeroproducts propellers were used on the F-82. They were full-feathering props because of the possibility that the aircraft might have to fly on one engine. The shape of a blade is shown here.

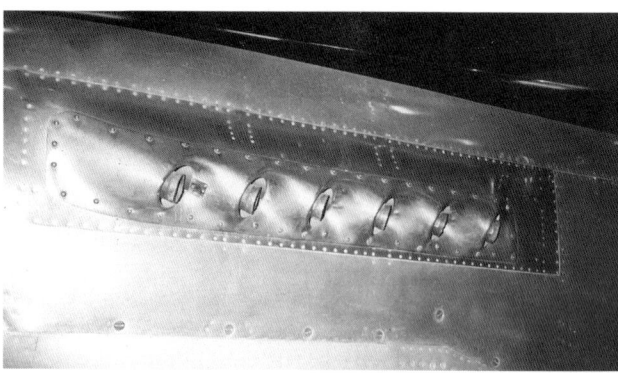

The exhausts on the P/F-82B, C, and D were similar to that seen on the P-51H. A streamlined housing covered the six ports on each side of the Merlin V-1650 engine. All other production Twin Mustangs were fitted with Allison engines and had different exhaust arrangements.

Details of the left canopy are shown here.

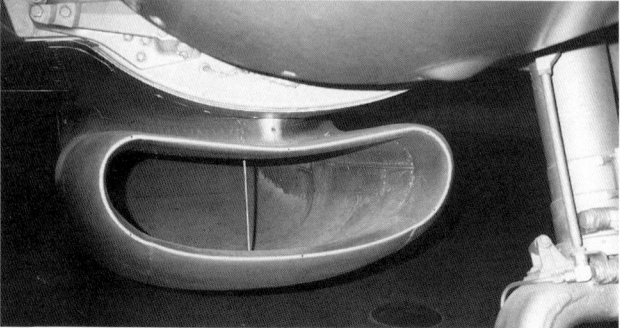

The antennas on the spines of the Twin Mustangs varied from one version to another. "Betty Jo" has ADF "football" antennas on both spines, but this was unusual. An antenna mast is also located on the spine of the right fuselage. Note the wire antennas in both photographs. Each enters the fuselage on the inboard side.

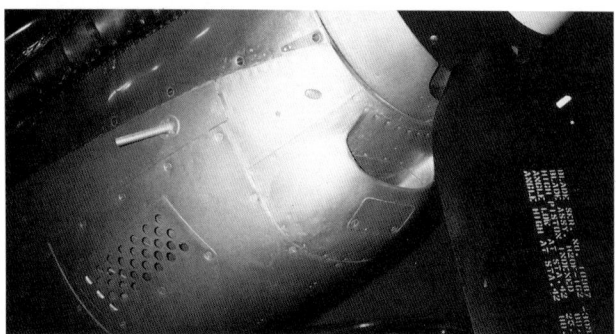

The carburetor scoop for one of the engines is shown at left, as is the perforated inspection panel for the air filter. This is the carburetor scoop as used on the XP-82, P-82B, P-82C, and P-82D. The carburetor scoop used on the Allison-powered Twin Mustangs, including the F-82E, F-82F, F-82G, and F-82H, was of a different design and was located further aft under the nose. The cooling-air intake is illustrated at right. Both of these photographs were taken on the left fuselage but were the same on the right side.

TAIL DETAILS

The large trim tab on the elevator can be seen in this view.

The two wire antennas connect to the vertical tails near the top as shown here.

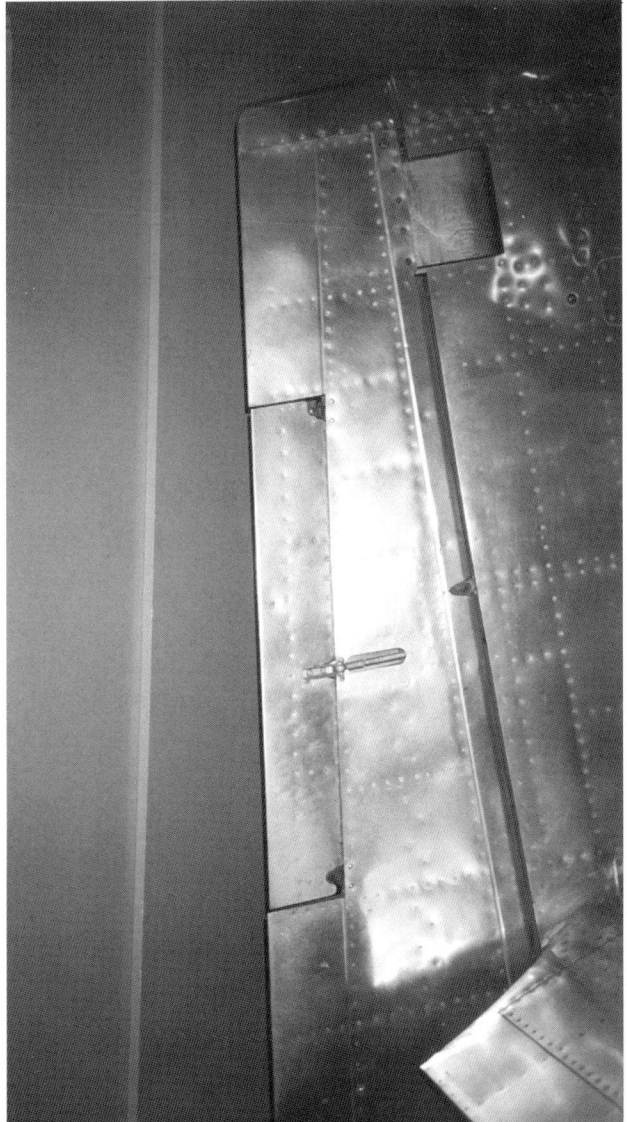

Each rudder had a trim tab that was controlled by an adjustment arm on the right side.

A white navigation light was located near the bottom of each rudder on the trailing edge.

MODELERS SECTION

Note: There have been scores of model kits of the P-51D Mustang produced. A full review of each would more than fill this entire publication. We are providing reviews of the models in 1/144th, 1/32nd, and 1/24th scales which were generally available as of October 1996. However, for 1/72nd and 1/48th scales, full reviews are included for what we consider the best four kits in each scale. For a few additional kits, very brief comments are also provided. Reviews for the Monogram 1/72nd scale and Modelcraft 1/48th scale P/F-82s are also included. We are limiting our coverage to the full production, injection-molded kits available from major manufacturers. Unfortunately, there are no injection-molded kits of the P-51H available from major model companies in any scale.

P-51 MUSTANG KITS

1/144th Scale Kits

<u>Arii P-51D Mustang, Kit Number 23032</u>

Although no longer generally available, this was one of only two P-51Ds that have been released in 1/144th scale. The kit best represents a Korean War F-51D with the cuffless Hamilton Standard propeller and under-wing rockets and bombs.

The surface scribing is raised and a bit on the heavy side. Once assembled, the model can be lightly sanded to bring the raised scribing down to a more acceptable level. The exhausts stand too proud from the fuselage, but it would be difficult to reduce them to the proper size.

Although the main landing gear struts and wheels are molded together, the doors are separate pieces. Neither the inner or outer doors are the correct shape, but some quick work with a file and sandpaper can correct this. The tail landing gear is a bit of a mystery. Half of it is molded as part of the right fuselage half, but there is no representation of the left half of the gear on the left fuselage or elsewhere in the kit.

The cockpit area is open, but there is no detailing. A seat and instrument panel made from plastic card would enhance the appearance of even this small model.

<u>Minicraft P-51D, Kit Number 4417</u>

Originally issued by Crown, this model is now marketed under the Minicraft label. Although it is supposed to be a P-51D, the kit provides the uncuffed Aeroproducts propeller used on the P-51K.

The recessed scribing is a little heavy, but not to the point it detracts from the overall appearance of the model. Main landing gear struts, wheels, and outer doors are molded as single units, but they are accurately represented and look good on the finished model. A separate set of landing gear doors is provided in the closed position for a gear-up "flying" model.

There is no cockpit detailing, and the appearance of the model will be significantly improved if the modeler takes a little time to add some details with plastic card.

The major shortcoming of the model is a lack of under-wing pylons and fuel tanks. We removed the pylons from a spare Revell 1/144th scale P-51B and added them to our review model. The external fuel tanks from the same kit can also be used on this model. We also used the Hamilton Standard propeller from the Revell kit to change this model from a P-51K to a P-51D.

1/72nd Scale Kits

<u>Airfix P-51D/K, Kit Number 02098</u>

Although it is older than the Hasegawa or Minicraft kits, it is still basically a good kit that can be used to produce a very nice model. However, the modeler will have to be ready to do a little more work to correct some problems. The plastic used is soft, and as a result, the details are not as crisp as they might be. The recessed panel lines are a little heavy but not overly so. They are not entirely accurate, but there are no major problems. The dorsal fin is solid, so it can easily be cut away if an early P-51D is to be built. The kit can also be used to build a P-51K, because Airfix included both the Hamilton Standard and Aeroproducts propellers.

The aileron and flaps are molded as part of the wing bottom, and this causes some fit problems when the two wing tops are glued in place. To solve one of these problems, we cut the flaps off and glued them in the lowered position. The gaps between the ailerons and the tops of the wings must be carefully filled and rescribed. The only other fit problem is where the wings join the fuselage. But some filling and sanding will eliminate the seams and gaps.

There is no detailing in the wheel wells, so we recommend building the model with the inner doors closed. The narrow part of each wheel well that remains exposed can be easily and quickly detailed if desired.

This 1/144th scale P-51D is the former Crown kit which is now marketed by Minicraft. The author used Chuck Yeager's markings on this model.

"Passion Wagon," which was flown by three different pilots, is the subject of this Airfix 1/72nd scale P-51D. It was built by the author.

Detailing on the cockpit sides is very well done for a 1/72nd scale kit. But the seat has a large ejector pin mark, and this should be removed. The instrument panel is not the correct shape, being too rounded at the top. The canopy and windscreen are molded as one piece, but they can easily be cut apart to display the interior of the cockpit if desired.

The hot air exhaust is molded in the closed position, and while this is not incorrect, the appearance of the model can be improved if some plastic card is used to show it open. There are some sink marks that need to be filled under the wings, and only 75-gallon tanks are provided as external stores. We replaced these with some extra 110-gallon tanks from a Hasegawa kit.

The exhausts and shrouds are too large and are mounted at too much of a downward angle. Some filing and reshaping will be needed here. The instructions and the locating ridge would have the modeler place the landing/taxi light at the front of the left wheel well. It should go at the rear of the well, and its shaft is about twice as long as it should be. Cut it in half before cementing it in place.

There are a lot of problems with this kit, but for the most part they are small ones that can be corrected easily. Our finished review sample is a nice addition to our 1/72nd scale, World War II, USAAF fighter collection.

Hasegawa P-51D, (Original Issue), Kit Numbers JS-101, 1101, and A012

These kits have been around for over twenty years, and they are identical except for the number of parts, color of the plastic, and decals provided. Depending on the kit, the prop shaft could be a separate part or molded as part of the nose piece.

Both shape and outline dimensions are very accurate, and panel lines are the fine raised type. The wings have the correct laminar flow profile, and this is seldom represented accurately on Mustang models. Likewise, the dihedral is correct. The windscreen is separate from the canopy, and both styles of canopies are included.

Small parts are accurately detailed and have crisp moldings. The main gear wells are the correct shape and depth and are adequately detailed for a 1/72nd scale model. However, the landing/taxi light that hangs down from the left well is missing. Two 75-gallon fuel tanks are provided for the under-wing pylons. The fabric represented on the rudder and elevators is too coarse, and most P-51Ds had metal elevators.

There is some detailing in the cockpit, but it is not very accurate. The features on the left side of the cockpit in particular should be reworked. Verlinden has a detailing set for this model that will be helpful in upgrading the cockpit. It also has a complete engine for modelers who want to add this feature to their model.

Fit is not as good as more recent Hasegawa kits. The ridges where the two fuselage halves are joined together must be sanded down, and some filling and sanding is needed where the wings join the fuselage.

Bill Slatton contributed to this review.

Hasegawa P-51D/K, (Newer Issue), Various Kit Numbers

This is not an updated version of the older kits covered above, but it is a completely different molding instead. The number of parts has more than doubled, providing better detailing and more options. Included in these options are parts to build both Hamilton Standard and Aeroproducts propellers, thereby allowing both a P-51D and P-51K to be built. Both 75-gallon and 110-gallon drop tanks are also provided as are shrouded and unshrouded exhausts. Also included in this kit is a landing/taxi light to go inside the left main gear well and the C-shaped brace to go inside the canopy frame.

Fit is excellent, and almost no filling or sanding is required. The scribing is delicate and recessed. Dimensions and shapes are all very accurate.

Detailing in the cockpit is better and more accurate than on the older kits, but the features on the sides are lacking. Some extra detailing will be required here if the canopy is to be displayed in the open position, and again, the Verlinden detail kit can be used. The canopy has the small roller where the antenna wire passes through it, but there is no hole through which the wire can be inserted.

On the negative side, the wheel wells are way too shallow, and we simply cannot understand why Hasegawa molded them this way. Clearly, there is plenty of room to mold them deep enough to look in scale. With the wings being molded on a separate tree, Hasegawa should certainly correct this problem for future releases. Another problem with the wing is that the dihedral is incorrect.

Bill Slatton used the original Hasegawa 1/72nd scale P-51D to build this model of LtCol. John C. Meyer's "Petie 2nd." (Slatton)

The later Hasegawa 1/72nd scale kit was also built by Bill Slatton. Kit decals were used on this model, and they are for "Jan," a P-51D from the 334th Fighter Squadron of the 4th Fighter Group. (Slatton)

Unlike the shallow wheel wells, this is easily corrected.

Bill Slatton contributed to this review.

Minicraft P-51D, Kit Number 2132

When originally issued, Minicraft's P-51D had a number of problems, not the least of which was that it had seven exhaust ports on each side. This new issue has the correct six ports and updated molding. It features engraved panel lines and raised details as well.

On first glance, this is a good kit. It has the best cockpit detailing of any 1/72nd scale Mustang and separate flaps that can be glued in the lowered position. But excellent detailing on the cockpit sides causes sink marks on the outside of both fuselage halves, so these must be filled and sanded. The fasteners on the cowling seem a bit too heavy when compared to the rest of the surface detail, and the holes in the air filter exhaust panels are raised instead of being recessed.

There is a noticeable shape problem where the fin fillet meets the vertical stabilizer. The leading edge of the stabilizer and the top of the fillet are too curved. These should be reshaped to the correct straight lines.

The wheel wells are deep enough to look in scale, and some detailing is provided. It isn't very accurate, and it would be best to glue the inner doors in the closed position. The wing does not have the correct dihedral, a fault common to many kits including the newer Hasegawa releases. This proved difficult to correct. The lower wing surfaces had to be cut completely through with a razor saw in two places in the inner wheel well area. Because it would be difficult to fill and sand the seams inside the wells, we again recommend gluing the inner doors in the closed position to cover the saw cuts.

The aerodynamic fairings just forward of the ailerons are present on the top of the wings, but are missing from the bottom. The shell ejector holes are too large, and the gun barrels all extend the same distance forward of the wing. The outer gun should extend the most, the center gun is about even with the wing, and the inner gun barrel ends inside the wing. The lights on the wing tips are round instead of being the correct teardrop shape.

The separate trailing edge flaps fit beautifully in the up position, but the leading edges of these assemblies are squared off instead of having a rounded airfoil shape. Hence, when positioned in the down pose, a big gap appears at the upper junction of the flap and wing. To correct this, the leading edges of the flaps must be sanded to the correct airfoil shape.

The spinner is too long and pointed. To fix this, sand the rear of the spinner backing plate down to about half its thickness. This will remove the shaft in the process. Glue the plate to the fuselage front, then cement the spinner (less the propeller blades) to it. Sand the front of the spinner to remove the "pointy-ness" and obtain an acceptable appearance. Finally, cut each propeller blade from the center piece that joins them together, and glue them separately into the spinner.

The landing gear is a little thick but basically acceptable. The tail wheel strut is too short and nearly disappears into its well when installed. A short piece of round sprue can be used to lengthen the strut.

Options include both 75 and 110-gallon drop tanks and both styles of canopies. Both are a bit too short in length and a little too tall. But when they are assembled in the open position, they look all right. The C-shaped brace that goes inside the canopy is included, but it is too high in profile.

With its excellent cockpit and dropped flaps, this kit can be used to build a very good model. It will just take extra work correcting shapes in several places and the dihedral of the wing to achieve acceptable results.

Walt Fink contributed to this review.

Matchbox P-51D

With a combination of raised and recessed panel lines, this kit is not the typical Matchbox offering. While it might look like a P-51D at first glance, it has noticeable shape problems. The nose section and spinner are particularly bad. The landing gear is not very accurate, and the aircraft sits too nose high. There is no detailing to speak of in the cockpit or wheel wells. Surface detailing, like the fairings in front of the ailerons, is also missing.

Walt Fink built Captain Raymond Wetmore's "Daddy's Girl" using the Minicraft P-51D in 1/72nd scale. A nice feature of this kit is the separate flaps. (Fink)

The author's son, Chip, used the Matchbox 1/72nd scale kit to built this model of Major Louis Norley's "Red Dog XII" for a sixth grade project on aviation history.

Heller P-51D, Kit Number 80268

With considerable shape, outline, and dimension

problems, this kit cannot be considered by the serious modeler. It lacks detailing in the cockpit and wheel wells, and what is provided is inaccurate.

Revell (Germany) P-51D, Kit number 04148

Of all P-51D kits presently available, this is the worst. There are major shape problems everywhere. For example, the inner main gear doors are rectangular in shape, while the outer doors are trapezoids. This model is so inaccurate that it cannot even be built as an acceptable desk stand model.

1/48th Scale Kits

Arii and Otaki P-51D, Various kit numbers

This model has been released by both Arii and Otaki, and in either case, we would rank it the fourth best P-51D in 1/48th scale. However, it falls short of the newer Tamiya and Hasegawa kits covered below.

The parts are molded in medium gray plastic and have engraved panel lines and countersunk rivets. Detailing in the cockpit and wheel wells is raised, but not very well defined. The canopy and windscreen are molded as a single piece, but could be cut apart if desired. A complete engine is provided with the appropriate mounts, and it can be viewed through a removable panel. Fit is generally good, with only a little filling and sanding being required.

When finished, this is a nice looking model, and it is one of the better kits from the 1970s. But it just does not measure up to the newer kits, especially when it comes to detailing.

Jim Roeder contributed to this review.

The Arii/Otaki P-51D is a good kit, but it is not up to the standards of the latest releases. This one was built with RAF markings by Jim Roeder. (Roeder)

Hasegawa P-51D/K, Various Kit Numbers

This excellent model ranks second only to the Tamiya kits among 1/48th scale models of the P-51D. It has been issued several times, with and without the fin fillet and with a variety of markings. On kits that have the fin fillet, it is thick enough that it can be removed easily and without leaving a hole in order to build an early P-51D without it. All molding is very crisp, and the engraved surface detailing is fine and accurate.

The kit contains 120 gray and 10 clear parts with

The excellent Hasegawa 1/48th scale model was built by Stan Parker. The markings are for "Delta Queen."
(Leggitt)

both styles of canopies being provided. Additionally, both the Hamilton Standard and Aeroproducts propellers are included, and this means that either a P-51D or P-51K can be built. The under-wing stores are the most extensive provided with any Mustang kit. They include 75 and 110-gallon drop tanks, two 500-pound bombs, M-10 triple 4.5-inch rocket tubes, and ten 5-inch rockets with appropriate launch rails. As a final option, shrouded and unshrouded exhausts are included.

The details in the wheel wells are effective but not completely accurate. Cockpit detailing is also reasonable, and it can be made to look very realistic with only proper painting and some wash to help bring out the highlights.

For many years, Hasegawa included the best and the most clear parts in their kits rather than expecting the modeler to paint the smaller glass parts silver. Unfortunately, they have recently gotten away from doing this, but this particular kit was released before the change. It offers several excellent details in the form of small clear pieces. The lens for the landing/taxi light, the navigation lights on the wing tips, and even the three identification lights under the right wing tip are separate clear pieces, and these add to the realism of the model. The lens portion of the K-14 gunsight is also a separate clear piece.

Many details that other model companies often mold as part of larger pieces are separate components in this kit. The scissors for the main gear struts, anti-sway braces for the bombs and fuel tanks, and the actuators for the inner gear doors are all individual parts. The interior of the cooling-air scoop, complete with the facing for the radiator, is also provided. The one area that is incorrect is the guns. Identical parts are provided as the ends of the gun barrels, and this would make each look the same as it projects forward of the wing's leading edge. But the outer two guns on each wing extend different lengths, and the inner gun does not extend forward of the wing at all. Fortunately, this is easy to correct.

Overall, this is an outstanding kit with excellent fit throughout. We highly recommend it.

Stan Parker contributed to this review.

Monogram P-51D, Various Kit Numbers

While not as good as the newer Hasegawa or Tamiya kits, this model could be called the best value of all P-51D models in 1/48th scale. Still selling for around $7.50 in 1996, this twenty-year old model is still very good and offers an option to the modeler on a budget.

Cockpit detailing is simple but effective. Even the wood grain is represented on the floor. The engraving on the instrument panel is exceptionally well done. Details on the cockpit sides are molded into the fuselage halves, and while this is not as desirable as having separate parts, it still looks very good on the finished model. Likewise, the detailing in the wheel wells looks very realistic.

The only optional parts in the kit are the shrouded and unshrouded exhausts. The only under-wing stores are 110-gallon fuel tanks. But Monogram did offer some open panels that reveal the underside of the engine compartment and the left gun bay. If built in the open position, these panels add features to the model that are particularly effective in the setting of a diorama. However, if the modeler chooses to cement these panels in a closed positions, there will be fit problems. The lower engine panel can be glued in place, and with considerable filling and sanding, the fit problem can be solved. This area should also be polished out if it is to be finished in natural metal. Doing an aircraft with a painted nose or a camouflage paint scheme will help. But the gun bay panels will be more difficult. Filling and sanding will remove the raised panel lines that should be there. There is no easy way to get a good fit with these panels closed, so it is easier just to assemble them in the open position. One hint that might prove helpful is to first remove the interior details that the engine and gun panels cover. This includes the ridge on the wing for the gun bay opening. Then glue the panels in place. For the gun bay doors, apply the cement from inside the wing.

The kit is fairly accurate except for the nose section. It is noticeably too wide, and this is most apparent when the model is viewed from the top. Unfortunately, there is very little that can be done to correct this problem.

This model does have its flaws, and it is not in the same class as the Hasegawa and Tamiya kits. But considering its age it is quite good. For modelers who want to avoid the high prices of the newer kits, this one is a good alternative.

Tamiya P-51D & F-51D, Kit Numbers 61040 & 61044

We rate these Tamiya kits as the best Mustang models in 1/48th scale, but it is a close call between this and the Hasegawa kit reviewed above. Hasegawa has better cockpit detailing and more options, while this kit has superior fit and flaps which are separate and can be easily assembled in the lowered position.

The difference between the P-51D and F-51D kits is more than just in the box art and decals. The F-51D kit (number 61044) has an additional sprue tree with a second propeller and ordnance. Tamiya misidentified the second propeller as being an Aeroproducts design, but it is the cuffless Hamilton Standard propeller used on P/F-51Ds late in their operational service. This is appropriate for most Korean War Mustangs. Additionally, there are two 250-pound bombs and six 5-inch rockets.

Both the P-51D and the F-51D kits provide the shrouded and unshrouded exhausts. Likewise, both styles of canopies are included, but this is where the optional parts end. Only the 75-gallon drop tanks are included.

Detailing inside the cooling-air scoop is excellent, but the inner part of the main gear wells is a separate piece. This results in seam lines inside the wells if the modeler is not very careful during construction. But with proper attention to this part of the assembly, these lines can be avoided. The wheel wells are deeper and more accurate than in any other Mustang in 1/48th scale.

Cockpit detailing leaves a bit to be desired, and we recommend replacing it with the True Details cockpit set which is designed specifically for these models. It is True Details Kit Number 48453.

Fit is superior to any other Mustang kit except for the spinner. Some filling and sanding will be required here, but once this is done, the four propeller blades will fit snugly in the holes even without the use of cement.

In addition to the canopies and windscreen, clear parts include the landing/taxi light and the gunsight. For both of these parts, the modeler is to paint the piece the appropriate color while leaving the light lens and the reflector in the gunsight clear. One negative with respect to the clear parts is that the two canopies are attached to the sprue tree in the clear area. This leaves a mark that must be sanded out, then polished. A corresponding mark

One of the best values in modeling is Monogram's 1/48th scale P-51D. It is the least expensive of all 1/48th scale Mustangs, and yet is a very good kit. The author built this one in the markings of Bud Anderson's "Old Crow."

The best 1/48th scale P-51D kit is the one from Tamiya. This model has the markings of "Margaret IV," and it was built by Lonnie Berry. (Munkasy)

is on the opposite side where there is an overflow cavity.

Tamiya is to be complimented for their way of using a plastic bushing to make sure the propeller spins, yet stays in place. It is simple and efficient.

Between the issue of the P-51D and F-51D kits, Tamiya changed to Scale-Master for their kit decals. Scale-Master, with their Invisa-clear process, makes the highest quality decals available to the modeler, and this is a big improvement over the decals in older Tamiya kits.

Lonnie Berry contributed to this review.

Revell P-51D, Kit Number H-31

If this kit was still commercially available, it would replace the Arii/Otaki kit as one of our four best P-51D Mustang models in 1/48th scale. It is basic, but it is accurate and well detailed for a model from the 1970s.

The raised panel lines are fine and accurate, and all major features of the P-51D are correctly represented. As a basic kit it could be preferred over the Monogram issue by modelers who do not care for the open engine and gun panels. Revell has been reissuing some of its older kits in limited "special products" releases, and we hope they will do it with this one. There is a place in today's market for a good, accurate, inexpensive Mustang in 1/48th scale.

Hawk/Testors P-51D, Various Kit Numbers

Originally released by Hawk, this kit is still available today from Testors. It has a mix of raised and engraved panel lines, and lacks detailing. However, the shape and outline are very accurate. As a basic model, this kit is a good value. The True Details cockpit set for the Tamiya kit can be made to fit these Hawk/Testors models if cockpit detailing is desired. Bombs, drop tanks, and three-tube rocket launchers are provided as under-wing stores. However, the rocket tubes are not represented as separate items on the undersides, so we suggest not using them.

Jim Roeder contributed to these comments.

Although not as well detailed as newer kits, the Testors P-51D is accurate in shape and outline. Jim Roeder built this one to represent Ernest Fiebelkorn's "Miss Miami." (Roeder)

Fujimi P-51D, Kit Number 5824

This kit has shape and outline problems. Detailing is not very accurate, and therefore we cannot recommend it. It does have an engine assembly with removable top cowl pieces. Some of these engine parts might be used on a Tamiya, Hasegawa, or Monogram model by a modeler who wants to open these areas up, but otherwise this kit is best left to the collectors. It was issued under Korea's Idea label and distributed by Hobbycraft of Canada as kit number 1514. However, this is not the same as the P-51D released under the Hobbycraft trademark.

Jim Roeder contributed to these comments.

Bob Bartolacci used the Fujimi 1/48th scale P-51D to build this model of "Passion Wagon." (Bartolacci)

Hobbycraft P-51D, Kit Number 1516

This kit is very similar to the Fujimi model covered above, but there are some notable differences. Fit is very poor, and detailing is inaccurate. There are shape and outline problems as well. We cannot recommend this kit to the serious scale modeler.

Jim Roeder contributed to these comments.

Jim Roeder used the Hobbycraft kit to build this P-51D in Brazilian markings. (Roeder)

1/32nd Scale Kits

Hasegawa P-51D, Various Kit Numbers

Although this kit has been around for over twenty years, it is still easily the best Mustang kit in 1/32nd scale

Among the best known of all P-51D markings are those for "The Millie P." They are shown here on a 1/32nd scale Hasegawa model built by Stan Parker. (Liggitt)

and one of the best in any scale. The model has a combination of raised and recessed panel lines that are accurate and very well executed. There is some fine rivet detail present, but it can easily be removed if desired. Both the rudder and the elevators are represented as having fabric covered surfaces, and although early P-51Ds did have fabric elevators, they were later replaced with ones having a metal skin. Those with fabric elevators were usually retrofitted. Therefore, we recommend sanding away the simulated fabric covering on the elevators.

Detail abounds everywhere. There is a complete engine that can be viewed through removable top cowl panels. This area can be enhanced with some tubing and wires as illustrated in the engine photographs on page 35 of this book. Both gun bays are open, and complete .50-caliber machine guns are included.

Cockpit detailing is pretty good except for the seat. Verlinden makes a detailing set that will help here. The Eduard detailing set can also be used to improve this area, and it also provides etched metal parts for the radiator and other features of the aircraft.

The wheel wells are enclosed and have some detailing. It is not as accurate nor complete as some of the more recent models, but it is adequate. Some modelers may prefer to glue the inner doors in the closed position rather than add any detailing to the inner sections of the wells. Under-wing stores include both 75 and 110-gallon tanks and 500-pound bombs.

The outline and shapes are accurate, and fit is generally good throughout. About the only problem with fit concerns installing the engine. There are no locating points, so it is hard to get the engine to seat firmly in a fixed position. Making some mounts from plastic card to go under the engine will help solve this problem. But otherwise, this model offers all the basics on which the super detailer can create a real masterpiece.

Stan Parker contributed to this review.

Revell P-51D, Kit Number

Although the fuselage and wing parts are obviously different, it appears that the fit and accuracy problems of Revell's 1/32nd scale P-51B were retained in this kit. The worst shape problem is that the cowling is too tapered as it was on the P-51B. The propeller blades are too thin, and the model is covered with rivets. There are wing pylons but no under-wing stores. The interior is inaccurate, because it is from the P-51B kit. Suffice it to say, the Hasegawa 1/32nd scale Mustang is far and away the better choice.

Jim Roeder contributed to these comments.

The Revell 1/32nd scale P-51D has many problems. It is not well detailed, and there are some inaccuracies with respect to shape and outline. It is also covered with large rivets. Jim Roeder built this model of "Willit Run?" straight from the box. (Roeder)

Monogram "Phantom" F-51D, Various Kit Numbers

Although this is not a kit that would normally be considered by the serious scale modeler, it is included here

Monogram's Phantom Mustang is considered a classic among plastic aircraft models. It was also issued in standard silver plastic without the control stand. This one was built by Josh Hairston, a junior modeler from Atlanta, Georgia.

because it is a true classic among plastic aircraft models. It has been released twice as a "phantom" model with clear parts that reveal the major interior components. A control stand is provided to operate the model's features. Motors spin the propeller and retract the landing gear, while a linkage drops the two bombs. It was also issued as a regular model in silver plastic, but it did not have the control stand, motors, and some of the interior parts.

The model most nearly represents a Korean War F-51D with the cuffless Hamilton Standard propeller. While the general shape and outline are accurate, and the cockpit detailing is quite good for a model that is now thirty years old, the working parts detract from its appeal as a truly accurate scale model. Most notable is that part of the linkage that retracts the main landing gear sticks through a slot in the bottom of the left wing.

Although it is not in the same class as the accurate and well-detailed models of today, this "phantom" model still has a different kind of appeal as a classic and as a demonstrator model. It is particularly interesting when it is painted on one side and left clear on the other.

1/24th Scale Kits

Airfix and MPC P-51D, Kit Numbers 14001 & 2-3505

Proving that bigger is not necessarily better, this kit offers more in quantity than quality. The poor molding and soft plastic result in a lot of parts that are warped, have a lot of flash, or don't fit well. Surface detailing is engraved, but it is too heavy and has some accuracy problems. There are numerous large rivets that must be sanded away.

The movable ailerons and elevators don't fit well, but the fit problems don't end there. A lot of filling and sanding will be required at almost every place pieces join together.

Detailing in the cockpit is very basic, but it is typical of that found in kits from the 1970s. In this scale, much additional work will be required to get it to look right. In particular, the seat will require some extra detailing.

The desire for working features caused Airfix to make the landing gear so it could be retracted. This results in more problems with fit and detailing. The main gear wells

A wide-angle lens provides an interesting effect for this large, 1/24th scale, Airfix P-51D. The model was built by Helge Lind, a modeler in Sweden who chose the markings of Col. John Lander's "Big Beautiful Doll" for his model.
(Ahlatrom)

are completely without detail, so their interiors will have to be built from scratch. Detailing the gear itself includes adding brake lines and towing rings as well as thinning the torque arms. The oleos are in the fully extended position as they would be in flight without any weight, so approximately one-eighth of an inch must be removed from each of them. Rubber tires are provided for all three wheels.

An engine is provided, and the basics are generally correct. But in this large scale, some detailing will be required. The same is true of the gun bays, both of which can be displayed in the open position. Bombs and 75-gallon fuel tanks are provided for the under-wing pylons, and six 5-inch rockets can also be added under the wings.

While this kit is fairly typical of one from the 1970s, it leaves a lot to be desired. It can be turned into a nice model, but considerable work, skill, and extra detailing will be required.

Helge Lind contributed to this review.

Bandai P-51D, Kit Number 0046782

Like the Airfix/MPC kit, this model offers more in the way of size than it does in excellence. Although it is a completely different kit rather than a copy, it offers many of the same features as the Airfix model. These include an engine which can be viewed through open panels, as well as open gun bays. Under-wing stores include 75-gallon tanks, 500-pound bombs, and 5-inch rockets. The rocket stubs are molded on the undersides of the wings and are not very accurate. The rockets themselves are even worse. The gun bays have only the basics, but they do have the novel option of having clear plastic cover panels. Panels molded in gray plastic are also provided.

The cockpit detailing is basic and not very accurate. A lot of work will be required to get it to look like the real thing. As with the Airfix/MPC kit, there is no detailing inside the main wheel wells. Rubber tires are likewise included in this kit.

Surface detailing is generally better than that found in the Airfix/MPC kit. Panel lines are recessed as are the rivets. Fit is not the best, and the modeler should be prepared to do a lot of filling and sanding during construction. Because the ailerons and elevators are molded as part of the wing and horizontal stabilizers respectively, they look much better than the separate parts on the Airfix/MPC model. The elevators are textured to look like they are fabric covered, but most P-51Ds had metal elevators. Those produced with fabric elevators were retrofitted with metal ones.

Some modelers may be lured by the large size of the 1/24th scale kits. But both the Airfix/MPC and this Bandai model will take a lot of work in the form of kit correcting, extra detailing, and filling and sanding to obtain an accurate and appealing model. The Hasegawa 1/32nd scale kit is far superior to both of these, and we recommend it as a much better alternative for modelers who want to build a large Mustang.

P/F-82 TWIN MUSTANG KITS

1/72nd Scale Kit

Monogram F-82, Kit Numbers 7501 & 6063

Originally released in 1973 as kit number 7501, this

The old Monogram kit is the only 1/72nd scale model available of the P/F-82. Al Lloyd built the black F-82G night fighter out of the box, and modified a second kit to build the silver F-82E. (Lloyd)

kit was reissued in 1984 in Monogram's Heritage Edition line as kit number 6063. In either case, it is identical, including the markings provided. It has also been released by Revell of Germany and under the Hobbycraft label.

Although quite accurate and relatively easy to assemble, the greatest difficulty during construction is assuring that all four landing gear wheels rest squarely on the ground. Optional features include a center wing gun bay which may be built in the opened or closed position, and several under-wing stores. The modeler may choose from drop tanks, two 250-pound bombs, or five 5-inch rockets on a "Christmas tree" launcher. The large radar housing for the F-82G's SCR-720 radar is also provided.

The kit is very well engineered. For example the propeller hubs and chin fairings may be installed at any point during the construction, while the propeller and spinner can be added after all painting is complete. This not only prevents possible breakage, it also greatly simplifies painting the propeller and spinner.

Although Monogram provided parts and markings to build both an F-82E escort fighter and an F-82G night fighter, the flame dampening exhausts that were common only to the night fighters are molded on the sides of each fuselage. Airwaves and DB Models produce resin nose sections for this kit with the proper exhausts for the F-82E.

Cockpit detailing is very sparse. For each cockpit, a single piece provides the floor, rudder pedals, and seat. A headrest, pilot figure, instrument panel, and control column is to be added to each. Detailing on the sides of each cockpit is represented only by scribing inside the fuselage halves. Therefore, most modelers will want to do some detailing here. Wheel well detail is decent for a 1/72nd scale model.

Surface scribing is raised, and it is a bit on the heavy side. It should be sanded down a little during assembly. Shape and outline are generally accurate except that the chord of the center wing section is too short by about an eighth of an inch.

Considering its age, this is not a bad kit. While it certainly is not up to models being released today, it still can be used to build a nice replica of the Twin Mustang.

Al Lloyd contributed to this review.

1/48th Scale Kit

<u>Modelcraft P-82B, F-82E, & F-82G, Various Kit Numbers</u>
Beginning in the summer of 1996, Modelcraft of Canada began releasing 1/48th scale kits of the Twin Mustang. First was the F-82E, and this was followed by the P-82B and F-82G. All are basically the same kit with different forward fuselage sections and other appropriate parts as required by the different variants.

The instructions are simple to the point that it is hard to determine just how and where some parts fit together. An example is the hot air exhaust in step 5. The view does not reveal that part C-8 actually slides over part C-7. Also, the actual shape of C-8 is considerably different than the illustration on the instructions.

These models are molded in the Czech Republic, and are crude by today's standards. The fit is the worst we have experienced on any kit we have ever reviewed. Almost every part will have to be filled, sanded, then refilled, and resanded where it joins with another part. Locating pins have to be removed in order to allow parts to join together properly. Additionally, the fuselage parts have small bumps on the mating edges in addition to the locating pins. The inside of the lower center wing section has two thick projections that have to be ground away before the upper part (A-5) will fit. We recommend test fitting parts several times while reworking them for a decent fit. These fit problems will be emphasized on the F-82E and P-82B models which have natural metal finishes.

One trick that will help with the fuselage halves is to disregard the kit instructions that tell the modeler to assemble the aft fuselage halves, then assemble the two forward fuselage halves to form the nose section, and finally join the two sections together. In trying a second kit, we found it easier to join the appropriate forward half to each aft fuselage half first, then glue the two completed fuselage halves together.

In assembling the tail wheels, it is necessary to reduce the height of the locating holes so that the tail wheels will be straight and the fuselage halves will meet without a gap. The pylons for the drop tanks have a poor fit to both the wings and the tanks. The stabilizer does not fit well either, and we recommend removing the locating pins and sanding the mating edges to correct this problem.

Detailing also leaves a lot to be desired. The cockpits are incomplete and not very accurate. The interiors of the main gear wells is detailed only with some ribs. Compare this to the photos on pages 59 and 60. Even the smaller and much older Monogram 1/72nd scale kit is considerably better. The series of oval holes on the underside of the wings is represented only by scribed lines. The fairings mounted just forward of the ailerons are missing.

Engineering of the kit is very poor. For example, one wonders why the fin caps are separate pieces when they should have been molded as part of the vertical stabilizers. This just adds more filling and sanding to the construction.

The shape and outline are fairly good, except that the center wing section is too short in chord. The trailing edge should be further aft.

We cannot recommend these kits because of their very poor fit. However, they are the only 1/48th scale Twin Mustangs that have been released to date. For any modeler determined to add a 1/48th scale F-82 to his collection, we suggest avoiding a natural metal finish by using the F-82G kit.

Jim Roeder contributed to this review.